Towards Gommecourt

Towards Gommecourt

Two accounts of British soldiers
on the Western Front during the
First World War

Attack
Edward G. D. Liveing

One Young Man
John Ernest Hodder-Williams

LEONAUR

Towards Gommecourt
Two accounts of British soldiers
on the Western Front during the
First World War
Attack by Edward G. D. Liveing
One Young Man by John Ernest Hodder-Williams

First published under the titles
Attack
and
One Young Man

Leonaur is an imprint of Oakpast Ltd

Copyright in this form © 2010 Oakpast Ltd

ISBN: 978-0-85706-120-1 (hardcover)
ISBN: 978-0-85706-119-5 (softcover)

http://www.leonaur.com

Publisher's Notes

In the interests of authenticity, the spellings, grammar and place names used have been retained from the original editions.

The opinions of the authors represent a view of events in which he was a participant related from his own perspective, as such the text is relevant as an historical document.

The views expressed in this book are not necessarily those of the publisher.

Contents

Attack

Edward G. D. Liveing

Contents

To

The N.C.O.S

And

Men of No. 5 Platoon

Of a Battalion of the County of London Regiment,

whom I had the good fortune to command in France
during 1915-1916,

and in particular to the memory

of RFN. C.N. Dennison My Platoon Observer,

who fell in action July 1st, 1916,

in an attempt to save my life

Introduction

The attack on the fortified village of Gommecourt, which Living describes in these pages with such power and colour, was a part of the first great allied attack on July 1, 1916, which began the battle of the Somme. That battle, so far as it concerns our own troops, may be divided into two sectors: one, to the south of the Ancre River, a sector of advance, the other, to the north of the Ancre River, a containing sector, in which no advance was possible. Gommecourt itself, which made a slight but important salient in the enemy line in the containing sector, was the most northern point attacked in that first day's fighting.

Though the Gommecourt position is not impressive to look at, most of our soldiers are agreed that it was one of the very strongest points in the enemy's fortified line on the Western Front. French and Russian officers, who have seen it since the enemy left it, have described it as "terrible" and as "the very devil." There can be no doubt that it was all that they say.

The country in that part is high-lying chalk downland, something like the downland of Berkshire and Buckinghamshire, though generally barer of trees, and less bold in its valleys. Before the war it was cultivated, hedgeless land, under corn and sugar-beet. The chalk is usually well-covered, as in Buckinghamshire, with a fat clay. As the French social tendency is all to the community, there are few lonely farms in that countryside as there would be with us. The inhabitants live in many compact villages, each with a church, a market-place, a watering-place for stock, and sometimes a *château* and park. Most of the villages are built of red brick, and the churches are of stone, not (as in the chalk countries with us) of dressed flint.

Nearly all the villages are planted about with orchards; some have copses of timber trees. In general, from any distance, the villages stand out upon the downland as clumps of woodland. Nearly everywhere near the battlefield a clump of orchard, with an occasional dark fir in it, is the mark of some small village. In time of peace the Picardy farming community numbered some two or three hundred souls. Gommecourt and Hébuterne were of the larger kind of village.

A traveller coming towards Gommecourt as Liveing came to it, from the west, sees nothing of the Gommecourt position till he reaches Hébuterne. It is hidden from him by the tilt of the high-lying chalk plateau, and by the woodland and orchards round Hébuterne village. Passing through this village, which is now deserted, save for a few cats, one comes to a fringe of orchard, now deep in grass, and of exquisite beauty. From the hedge of this fringe of orchard one sees the Gommecourt position straight in front, with the Gommecourt salient curving round on slightly rising ground, so as to enclose the left flank.

At first sight the position is not remarkable. One sees, to the left, a slight rise or swelling in the chalk, covered thickly with the remains and stumps of noble trees, now mostly killed by shell-fire. This swelling, which is covered with the remains of Gommecourt Park, is the salient of the enemy position. The enemy trenches here jut out into a narrow pointing finger to enclose and defend this slight rise.

Further to the right, this rise becomes a low, gentle heave in the chalk, which stretches away to the south for some miles, becoming lower and gentler in its slope as it proceeds. The battered woodland which covers its higher end contains the few stumps and heaps of brick that were once Gommecourt village. The lower end is without trees or buildings.

This slight wooded rise and low, gentle heave in the chalk make up the position of Gommecourt. It is nothing but a gentle rise above a gentle valley. From a mile or two to the south of Gommecourt, this valley appearance becomes more marked. If one looks northward from this point the English lines seem to follow a slight rise parallel with the other. The valley between the two heaves of chalk make the No Man's Land or space between the enemy trenches and our own. The salient shuts in the end of the valley and enfilades it.

The position has changed little since the attack of July 1. Then, as now, Gommecourt was in ruins, and the trees of the wood were mostly killed. Then, as now, the position looked terrible, even though its slopes were gentle and its beauty not quite destroyed, even after two years of war.

The position is immensely strong in itself, with a perfect glacis and field of fire. Every invention of modern defensive war helped to make it stronger. In front of it was the usual system of barbed wire, stretched on iron supports, over a width of fifty yards. Behind the wire was the system of the First Enemy Main Line, from which many communication-trenches ran to the central fortress of the salient, known as the Kern Redoubt, and to the Support or Guard Line. This First Main Line, even now, after countless bombardments and nine months of neglect, is a great and deep trench of immense strength. It is from twelve to fifteen feet deep, very strongly revetted with timberings and stout wicker-work.

At intervals it is strengthened with small forts or sentry-boxes of concrete, built into the parapet. Great and deep dugouts lie below it, and though many of these have now been destroyed, the shafts of most of them can still be seen. At the mouths of some of these shafts one may still see giant-legged periscopes by which men sheltered in the dug-out shafts could watch for the coming of an attack. When the attack began and the barrage lifted, these watchers called up the bombers and machine-gunners from their underground barracks, and had them in action within a few seconds.

Though the wire was formidable and the trench immense, the real defences of the position were artillery and machine-guns. The machine-guns were the chief danger. One machine-gun with ample ammunition has concentrated in itself the defensive power of a battalion. The enemy had not less than a dozen machine-guns in and in front of the Kern Redoubt. Some of these were cunningly hidden in pits, tunnels and shelters in (or even outside) the obstacle of the wire at the salient, so that they could enfilade the No Man's Land, or shoot an attacking party in the back after it had passed. The sites of these machine-gun nests were well hidden from all observation, and were frequently changed.

Besides the machine-guns outside and in the front line, there were others, mounted in the trees and in the higher ground above the front line, in such position that they, too, could play upon the No Man's Land and the English front line. The artillery concentrated behind Gommecourt was of all calibres. It was a greater concentration than the enemy could then usually afford to defend any one sector, but the number of guns in it is not known. On July 1 it developed a more intense artillery fire upon Hébuterne, and the English line outside it, than upon any part of the English attack throughout the battlefield.

In the attack of July 1, Gommecourt was assaulted simultaneously from the north (from the direction of Fonquevillers) and from the south (from the direction of Hébuterne). Liveing took part in the southern assault, and must have "gone in" near the Hébuterne-Bucquoy Road. The tactical intention of these simultaneous attacks from north and south was to "pinch off" and secure the salient. The attack to the north, though gallantly pushed, was unsuccessful. The attack to the south got across the first-line trench and into the enemy position past Gommecourt Cemetery almost to the Kern Redoubt. What it faced in getting so far may be read in Liveing's account. Before our men left the trenches outside Hébuterne they were in a heavy barrage, and the open valley of the No Man's Land hissed, as Liveing says, like an engine, with machine-gun bullets. Nevertheless, our men reached the third line of enemy trenches and began to secure the ground which they had captured.

During the afternoon the enemy counter-attacked from the south, and, later in the day, from the north as well. Our men had not enough bombs to hold back the attackers, and were gradually driven back, after very severe hand-to-hand fighting in the trenches, to an evil little bend in the front line directly to the south of Gommecourt Cemetery. At about 11 p.m., after sixteen hours of intense and bitter fighting, they were driven back from this point to their own lines.

CHAPTER 1

Gathering for Attack

The roads were packed with traffic. Column after column of lorries came pounding along, bearing their freight of shells, trench-mortar bombs, wire, stakes, sandbags, pipes, and a thousand other articles essential for the offensive, so that great dumps of explosives and other material arose in the green wayside places. Staff cars and signallers on motor-bikes went busily on their way. Ambulances hurried backwards and forwards between the line and the Casualty Clearing Station, for the days of June were hard days for the infantry who dug the "leaping-off" trenches, and manned them afterwards through rain and raid and bombardment. Horse transport and new batteries hurried to their destinations. "Caterpillars" rumbled up, towing the heavier guns. Infantrymen and sappers marched to their tasks round and about the line.

Roads were repaired, telephone wires placed deep in the ground, trees felled for dugouts and gun emplacements, water-pipes laid up to the trenches ready to be extended across conquered territory, while small-gauge and large-gauge railways seemed to spring to being in the night.

Then came days of terror for the enemy. Slowly our guns broke forth upon them in a tumult of rage. The Germans in retaliation sprayed our nearer batteries with shrapnel, and threw a barrage of whizz-bangs across the little white road leading into the village of Hébuterne. This feeble retaliation was swallowed up and overpowered by the torrent of metal that now poured incessantly into their territory. Shells from the 18-pounders and trench-mortars cut their wire and demoralised their sentries. Guns of all calibres pounded their system of trenches till it looked for all the world like nothing more than a ploughed field. The sky was filled with our aeroplanes wheeling about and directing the work of batteries, and with the black and white bursts of anti-aircraft shells. Shells from the 9.2 howitzers crashed into strong points and gun emplacements and hurled them skywards. Petrol shells licked up the few remaining green-leaved trees in Gommecourt Wood, where observers watched and snipers nested: 15-inch naval guns, under the vigilant guidance of observation balloons, wrought deadly havoc in Bapaume and other villages and billets behind their lines.

Thrice were the enemy enveloped in gas and smoke, and, as they stood-to in expectation of attack, were mown down by a torrent of shells.

The bombardment grew and swelled and brought down showers of rain. Yet the ground remained comparatively dry and columns of dust arose from the roads as hoof and wheel crushed their broken surfaces and battalions of infantry, with songs and jests, marched up to billets and bivouacs just behind the line, ready to give battle.

CHAPTER 2

Eve of Attack

Boom! Absolute silence for a minute. Boom! followed quickly by a more distant report from a fellow-gun. At each bellowing roar from the 9.2 nearby, bits of the ceiling clattered on to the floor of the billet and the wall-plaster trickled down on to one's valise, making a sound like soot coming down a chimney.

It was about three o'clock in the morning. I did not look at my watch, as its luminous facings had faded away months before and I did not wish to disturb my companions by lighting a match. A sigh or a groan came from one part of the room or another, showing that our bombardment was troublesome even to the sleepers, and a rasping noise occasionally occurred when W——k, my Company Commander, turned round uneasily on his bed of wood and rabbit-wire.

I plunged farther down into the recesses of my flea-bag, though its linings had broken down and my feet stuck out at the bottom. Then I pulled my British Warm over me and muffled my head and ears in it to escape the regularly-repeated roar of the 9.2. Though the whole house seemed to be shaking to bits at every minute, the noise was muffled to a less ear-splitting fury and I gradually sank into a semi-sleep.

About six o'clock I awoke finally, and after an interval the battery stopped its work. At half-past seven I hauled myself out of my valise and sallied forth into the courtyard, clad in a British Warm, pyjamas, and gum-boots, to make my toilet. I blinked as I came into the light and felt very sleepy. The next moment I was on my hands and knees, with every nerve of my brain working like a mill-stone. A vicious "swish" had sounded over my head, and knowing its meaning I had turned for the nearest door and slipped upon the cobbled stones of the yard. I picked myself up and fled for that door just as the inevitable "crash" came. This happened to be the door to the servants' quarters, and they were vastly amused. We looked out of the window at the *débris* which was rising into the air. Two more "crumps" came whirling over the house, and with shattering explosions lifted more *débris* into the air beyond the farther side of the courtyard. Followed a burst of shrapnel and one more "crump," and the enemy's retaliation on the 9.2 and its crew had ceased. The latter, however, had descended into their dug-out, while the gun remained unscathed. Not so some of our own men.

We were examining the nose-cap of a shell which had hit the wall of our billet, when a corporal came up, who said hurriedly to W——k, "Corporal G——'s been killed and four men wounded."

The whole tragedy had happened so swiftly, and this sudden announcement of the death of one of our best N.C.O.s had come as such a shock, that all we did was to stare at each other with the words:

"My God! Corporal G—— gone! It's impossible."

One expects shells and death in the line, but three or four miles behind it one grows accustomed, so to speak, to live in a fool's paradise. We went round to see our casualties, and I found two of my platoon, bandaged in the leg and arm, sitting in a group of their pals, who were congratulating them on having got "soft Blighty ones." The Company Quartermaster-Sergeant showed me a helmet, which was lying outside the billet when the shells came over, with a triangular gash in it, into which one could almost place one's fist. At the body of Corporal G—— I could not bring myself to look. The poor fellow had been terribly hit in the back and neck, and, I confess it openly, I had not the courage, and felt that it would be a sacrilege, to gaze on the mangled remains of one whom I had valued so much as an N.C.O. and grown to like so much as a man during the last ten months.

Dark clouds were blowing over in an easterly direction; a cheerless day added to the general gloom. We had a Company Officers' final consultation on the plans for the morrow, after which I held an inspection of my platoon, and gave out some further orders. On my return to the billet W——k told me that the attack had been postponed for two days owing to bad weather. Putting aside all thought of orders for the time being, we issued out rum to the men, indulged in a few "tots" ourselves, and settled down to a pleasant evening.

★ ★ ★ ★ ★

In a little courtyard on the evening of June 30 I called the old platoon to attention for the last time, shook hands with the officers left in reserve, marched off into the road, and made up a turning to the left on to the Blue Track. We had done about a quarter of the ground between Bayencourt and Sailly-au-Bois when a messenger hurried up to tell me to halt, as several of the platoons of the L—— S—— had to pass us. We sat down by a large shell-hole, and the men lit up their pipes and cigarettes and shouted jokes to the men of the other regiment as they passed by.

It was a very peaceful evening—remarkably peaceful, now that the guns were at rest. A light breeze played eastward. I sat with my face towards the sunset, wondering a little if this was the last time that I should see it. One often reads of this sensation in second-rate novels. I must say that I had always thought it greatly "overdone"; but a great zest in the splendour of life swept over me as I sat there in the glow of that setting sun, and also a great calmness that gave me heart to do my uttermost on the morrow. My father had enclosed a little card in his last letter to me with the words upon it of the prayer of an old cavalier of the seventeenth century—Sir Jacob Astley—before the battle of Newbury:—*Lord, I shall be very busy this day. I may forget Thee, but do not Thou forget me.* A peculiar old prayer, but I kept on repeating it to myself with great comfort that evening.

My men were rather quiet. Perhaps the general calmness was affecting them with kindred thoughts, though an Englishman never shows them. On the left stood the stumpy spire of Bayencourt Church just left by us. On the right lay Sailly-au-Bois in its girdle of trees. Along the side of the valley which ran out from behind Sailly-au-Bois, arose numerous lazy pillars of smoke from the wood fires and kitchens of an artillery encampment. An English aeroplane, with a swarm of black puffs around it betokening German shells, was gleaming in the setting sun. It purred monotonously, almost drowning the screech of occasional shells which were dropping by a distant *château*. The calm before the storm sat brooding over everything.

The kilted platoons having gone on their way, we resumed our journey, dipping into the valley behind Sailly-au-Bois, and climbing the farther side, as I passed the officers' mess hut belonging to an anti-aircraft battery, which had taken up a position at the foot of the valley, and whence came a pleasant sound of clinking glass, a wild desire for permanent comfort affected me.

Bounding the outskirts of Sailly-au-Bois, we arrived in the midst of the battery positions nesting by the score in the level plain behind Hébuterne. The batteries soon let us know of their presence. Red flashes broke out in the gathering darkness, followed by quick reports.

To the right one could discern the dim outlines of platoons moving up steadily and at equal distances like ourselves. One could just catch the distant noise of spade clinking on rifle. When I turned my gaze to the front of these troops, I saw yellow-red flashes licking upon the horizon, where our shells were finding their mark. Straight in front, whither we were bound, the girdle of trees round Hébuterne shut out these flashes from view, but by the noise that came from beyond those trees one knew that the German trenches were receiving exactly the same intensity of fire there. Every now and then this belt of trees was being thrown into sharp relief by German star-shells, which rocketed into the sky one after the other like a display of fireworks, while at times a burst of hostile shrapnel would throw a weird, red light on the twinkling poplars which surrounded the cemetery.

As we marched on towards the village (I do not mind saying it) I experienced that unpleasant sensation of wondering whether I should be lying out this time tomorrow—stiff and cold in that land beyond the trees, where the red shrapnel burst and the star-shells flickered. I remember hoping that, if the fates so decreed, I should not leave too great a gap in my family, and, best hope of all, that I should instead be speeding home in an ambulance on the road that stretched along to our left. I do not think that I am far wrong when I say that those thoughts were occurring to every man in the silent platoon behind me. Not that we were downhearted. If you had asked the question, you would have been greeted by a cheery "No!" We were all full of determination to do our best next day, but one cannot help enduring rather an unusual "party feeling" before going into an attack.

Suddenly a German shell came screaming towards us. It hurtled overhead and fell behind us with muffled detonation in Sailly-au-Bois. Several more screamed over us as we went along, and it was peculiar to hear the shells of both sides echoing backwards and forwards in the sky at the same time.

We were about four hundred yards from the outskirts of Hébuterne, when I was made aware of the fact that the platoon in front of me had stopped. I immediately stopped my platoon. I sat the men down along a bank, and we waited—a wait which was whiled away by various incidents. I could hear a dog barking, and just see two gunner officers who were walking unconcernedly about the battery positions and whistling for it. The next thing that happened was a red flash in the air about two hundred yards away, and a pinging noise as bits of shrapnel shot into the ground round about. One of my men, S—— (the poor chap was killed next day), called to me: "Look at that fire in Sailly, sir!" I turned round and saw a great yellow flare illuminating the sky in the direction of Sailly, the fiery end of some barn or farm-building, where a high explosive had found its billet.

We remained in this spot for nearly a quarter of an hour, after which R——d's platoon began to move on, and I followed at a good distance with mine. We made our way to the clump of trees over which the shrapnel had burst a few minutes before. Suddenly we found ourselves floundering in a sunken road flooded with water knee-deep. This was not exactly pleasant, especially when my guide informed me that he was not quite certain as to our whereabouts. Luckily, we soon gained dry ground again, turned off into a bit of trench which brought us into the village, and made for the dump by the church, where we were to pick up our materials. When we reached the church—or, rather, its ruins—the road was so filled with parties and platoons, and it was becoming so dark, that it took us some time before we found the dump. Fortunately, the first person whom I spotted was the Regimental Sergeant-Major, and I handed over to him the carrying-party which I had to detail, also despatching the rum and soup parties—the latter to the company cooker.

Leaving the platoon in charge of Sergeant S——l, I went with my guide in search of the dump. In the general *mêlée* I bumped into W——k. We found the rabbit wire, barbed wire, and other material in a shell-broken outhouse, and, grabbing hold of it, handed the stuff out to the platoon.

As we filed through the village the reflections of star-shells threw weird lights on half-ruined houses; an occasional shell screamed overhead, to burst with a dull, echoing sound within the shattered walls of former cottages; and one could hear the rat-tat-tat of machine-guns. These had a nasty habit of spraying the village with indirect fire, and it was, as always, a relief to enter the recesses of Wood Street without having any one hit. This communication trench dipped into the earth at right angles to the "Boulevard" Street. We clattered along the brick-floored trench, whose walls were overhung with the dewy grass and flowers of the orchard—that wonderful orchard whose aroma had survived the horror and desolation of a two years' warfare, and seemed now only to be intensified to a softer fragrance by the night air.

Arriving at the belt of trees and hedge which marked the confines of the orchard, we turned to the right into Cross Street, which cut along behind the belt of trees into Woman Street.

Turning to the left up Woman Street, and leaving the belt of trees behind, we wound into the slightly undulating ground between Hébuterne and Gommecourt Wood. "Crumps" were bursting round about the communication trench, but at a distance, judging by their report, of at least fifty yards. As we were passing Brigade Headquarters' Dug-out, the Brigade-Major appeared and asked me the number of my platoon. "Number 5," I replied; and he answered "Good," with a touch of relief in his voice—for we had been held up for some time on the way, and my platoon was the first or second platoon of the company to get into the line.

It was shortly after this that "crumps" began to burst dangerously near. There was suddenly a blinding flash and terrific report just to our left. We kept on, with heads aching intolerably. Winding round a curve, we came upon the effects of the shells. The sides of the trench had been blown in, while in the middle of the *débris* lay a dead or unconscious man, and farther on a man groaning faintly upon a stretcher. We scrambled over them, passed a few more wounded and stretcher-bearers, and arrived at the Reserve Line.

Captain W———t was standing at the juncture of Woman Street and the Reserve Line, cool and calm as usual. I asked him if New Woman Street was blocked, but there was no need for a reply. A confused noise of groans and stertorous breathing, and of someone sobbing, came to my ears, and above it all, M——— W———'s voice saying to one of his men: "It's all right, old chap. It's all over now." He told me afterwards that a shell had landed practically in the trench, killing two men in front of him and one behind, and wounding several others, but not touching himself.

It was quite obvious to me that it was impossible to proceed to the support trench via New Woman Street, and at any rate my Company Commander had given me orders to go over the top from the reserve to the support line, so, shells or no shells, and leaving Sergeant S———l to bring up the rear of the platoon, I scaled a ladder leaning on the side of the trench and walked over the open for about two hundred yards. My guide and I jumped into New Woman Street just before it touched the support line, and we were soon joined by several other men of the platoon. We had already suffered three casualties, and going over the top in the darkness, the men had lost touch. The ration party also had not arrived yet. I despatched the guide to bring up the remainder, and proceeded to my destination with about six men. About fifteen yards farther up the trench I found a series of shell-holes threading their way off to the left. By the light of some German star-shells I discerned an officer groping about these holes, and I stumbled over mounds and hollows towards him.

"Is this the support line?" I asked, rather foolishly.

"Yes," he replied, "but there isn't much room in it." I saw that he was an officer of the Royal Engineers.

"I'm putting my smoke-bombers down here," he continued, "but you'll find more room over towards the sunken road."

He showed me along the trench—or the remains of it—and went off to carry out his own plans. I stumbled along till I could just distinguish the outlines of the sunken road. The trench in this direction was blown in level with the ground. I returned to W——k, whose headquarters were at the juncture of New Woman Street and the support line, telling him that the trench by the sunken road was untenable, and that I proposed placing my platoon in a smaller length of trench, and spreading them out fanwise when we started to advance. To this he agreed, and putting his hand on my shoulder in his characteristic fashion, informed me in a whisper that the attack was to start at 7.30 a.m. As far as I can remember it was about one o'clock by now, and more of my men had come up. I ensconced them by sections. No. 1 section on the left and No. 4 on the right in shell-holes and the remains of the trench along a distance of about forty yards, roughly half the length of the trench that they were to have occupied. At the same time I gave orders to my right-and left-hand guides to incline off to the right and left respectively when the advance started. I was walking back to my headquarters, a bit of trench behind a traverse, when a German searchlight, operating from the direction of Serre Wood, turned itself almost dead on me. I was in my trench in a second.

Shortly afterwards Sergeant S——r arrived with No. 8 platoon. I showed him one or two available portions of trench, but most of his men had to crowd in with mine. The Lewis-gunners, who arrived last, found only a ruined bit of trench next to my "headquarters," while they deposited their guns and equipment in a shell-hole behind.

It was somewhere about four or half-past when I made my last inspection. I clambered over the back of the trench and stood still for a moment or so. Everything was uncannily silent. There was just a suspicion of whiteness creeping into the sky beyond the rising ground opposite. Over towards the left rose the remains of Gommecourt Wood.

Half its trees had gone since the last time that I had seen it, and the few that remained stood, looking like so many masts in a harbour, gaunt and charred by our petrol shells.

The men in the left fire-bay seemed quite comfortable. But, standing and looking down the trench, it suddenly dawned upon me that I was gazing right into a line of chalky German trenches, and consequently that the enemy in those trenches could look straight into this trench. I left instructions with the corporal in charge of that section to build up a barricade in the gap before daybreak. As I went along the rest of our frontage, Sergeant S——l doled out the rum.

I retired to my "headquarters," but not so Sergeant S——l, who seemed not to bother a bit about the increasing light and the bullets which came phitting into the ground in rather an unpleasant quantity. I was glad when I had finally got him down into the trench. W——k had also told him to get in, for he remarked—

"Captain W——k, 'e says to me, 'Get into the trench, S——l, you b—— fool!' so I've got in."

He was just in time. A prelude of shrapnel screamed along, bursting overhead, and there followed an hour's nerve-racking bombardment.

CHAPTER 3

Attack

Dawn was breaking. The morning was cool after a chill night—a night of waiting in blown-down trenches with not an inch to move to right or left, of listening to the enemy's shells as they left the guns and came tearing and shrieking towards you, knowing all the time that they were aimed for your particular bit of trench and would land in it or by it, of awaiting that sudden, ominous silence, and then the crash—perhaps death.

I, for my part, had spent most of the night sitting on a petrol tin, wedged between the two sides of the trench and two human beings-my sergeant on the left and a corporal on the right. Like others, I had slept for part of the time despite the noise and danger, awakened now and then by the shattering crash of a shell or the hopeless cry for stretcher-bearers.

But morning was coming at last, and the bombardment had ceased. The wind blew east, and a few fleecy clouds raced along the blue sky overhead. The sun was infusing more warmth into the air. There was the freshness and splendour of a summer morning over everything. In fact, as one man said, it felt more as if we were going to start off for a picnic than for a battle.

"Pass it down to Sergeant H—— that Sergeant S——l wishes him the top o' the mornin'," said my sergeant. But Sergeant H——, who was in charge of the company's Lewis-guns, and had been stationed in the next fire-trench, was at present groping his way to safety with a lump of shrapnel in his back.

An occasional shell sang one way or the other. Otherwise all was quiet. We passed down the remains of the rum. Sergeant S——l pressed me to take some out of a mess-tin lid. I drank a very little—the first and last "tot" I took during the battle. It warmed me up. Sometime after this I looked at my watch and found it was a minute or two before 6.25 a.m. I turned to the corporal, saying—

"They'll just about start now."

The words were not out of my mouth before the noise, which had increased a trifle during the last twenty minutes, suddenly swelled into a gigantic roar. Our guns had started. The din was so deafening that one could not hear the crash of German shells exploding in our own lines.

Sergeant S——l was standing straight up in the trench and looking over to see the effects of our shells. It was a brave thing to do, but absolutely reckless. I pulled him down by the tail of his tunic. He got up time and again, swearing that he would "take on the whole b— German army." He gave us pleasing information of the effects of our bombardment, but as I did not want him to lose his life prematurely, I saw to it that we kept him down in the trench till the time came for a display of bravery, in which he was not lacking.

We had been told that the final bombardment that day would be the most intense one since the beginning of the war. The attack was to encircle what was almost generally considered the strongest German "fortress" on the Western Front, the stronghold of Gommecourt Wood. There was need of it, therefore.

Just over the trenches, almost raising the hair on one's head (we were helmeted, I must say, but that was the feeling), swished the smaller shells from the French .75 and English 18-pounder batteries. They gave one the sensation of being under a swiftly rushing stream. The larger shells kept up a continuous shrieking overhead, falling on the enemy's trenches with the roar of a cataract, while every now and then a noise as of thunder sounded above all when our trench-mortar shells fell amongst the German wire, blowing it to bits, making holes like mine craters, and throwing dirt and even bits of metal into our own trenches.

I have often tried to call to memory the intellectual, mental and nervous activity through which I passed during that hour of hellish bombardment and counter-bombardment, that last hour before we leapt out of our trenches into No Man's Land. I give the vague recollection of that ordeal for what it is worth. I had an excessive desire for the time to come when I could go "over the top," when I should be free at last from the noise of the bombardment, free from the prison of my trench, free to walk across that patch of No Man's Land and opposing trenches till I got to my objective, or, if I did not go that far, to have my fate decided for better or for worse.

I experienced, too, moments of intense fear during close bombardment. I felt that if I was blown up it would be the end of all things so far as I was concerned. The idea of after-life seemed ridiculous in the presence of such frightful destructive force. Again the prayer of that old cavalier kept coming to my mind. At any rate, one could but do one's best, and I hoped that a higher power than all that which was around would not overlook me or any other fellows on that day.

At one time, not very long before the moment of attack, I felt to its intensest depth the truth of the proverb, *Carpe diem*. What was time? I had another twenty minutes in which to live in comparative safety. What was the difference between twenty minutes and twenty years? Really and truly what was the difference? I was living at present, and that was enough. I am afraid that this working of mind will appear unintelligible. I cannot explain it further. I think that others who have waited to "go over" will realise its meaning. Above all, perhaps, and except when shells falling nearby brought one back to reality, the intense cascade-like noise of our own shells rushing overhead numbed for the most part of the time one's nervous and mental system. Listening to this pandemonium, one felt like one of an audience at a theatre and not in the least as if one was in any way associated with it oneself.

Still, the activity of a man's nerves, though dulled to a great extent inwardly, were bound to show externally. I turned to the corporal. He was a brave fellow, and had gone through the Gallipoli campaign, but he was shaking all over, and white as parchment. I expect that I was just the same.

"We must be giving them hell," I said. "I don't think they're sending much back."

"I don't think much, sir," he replied.

I hardly think we believed each other. Looking up out of the trench beyond him, I saw huge, black columns of smoke and *débris* rising up from our communication trench. Then, suddenly, there was a blinding "crash" just by us. We were covered in mud which flopped out of the trench, and the evil-smelling fumes of lyddite. The cry for stretcher-bearers was passed hurriedly up the line again. Followed "crash" after "crash," and the pinging of shrapnel which flicked into the top of the trench, the purring noise of flying nose-caps and soft thudding sounds as they fell into the parapet.

It was difficult to hear one another talking. Sergeant S——l was still full of the "get at 'em" spirit. So were we all. The men were behaving splendidly. I passed along the word to "Fix swords."

We could not see properly over the top of the trench, but smoke was going over. The attack was about to begin—it was beginning. I passed word round the corner of the traverse, asking whether they could see if the second wave was starting. It was just past 7.30 a.m. The third wave, of which my platoon formed a part, was due to start at 7.30 plus 45 seconds—at the same time as the second wave in my part of the line. The corporal got up, so I realised that the second wave was assembling on the top to go over. The ladders had been smashed or used as stretchers long ago. Scrambling out of a battered part of the trench, I arrived on top, looked down my line of men, swung my rifle forward as a signal, and started off at the prearranged walk.

A continuous hissing noise all around one, like a railway engine letting off steam, signified that the German machine-gunners had become aware of our advance. I nearly trod on a motionless form. It lay in a natural position, but the ashen face and fixed, fearful eyes told me that the man had just fallen. I did not recognise him then. I remember him now. He was one of my own platoon.

To go back for a minute. The scene that met my eyes as I stood on the parapet of our trench for that one second is almost indescribable. Just in front the ground was pitted by innumerable shell-holes. More holes opened suddenly every now and then. Here and there a few bodies lay about. Farther away, before our front line and in No Man's Land, lay more. In the smoke one could distinguish the second line advancing. One man after another fell down in a seemingly natural manner, and the wave melted away. In the background, where ran the remains of the German lines and wire, there was a mass of smoke, the red of the shrapnel bursting amid it.

Amongst it, I saw Captain H—— and his men attempting to enter the German front line. The Boches had met them on the parapet with bombs. The whole scene reminded me of battle pictures, at which in earlier years I had gazed with much amazement. Only this scene, though it did not seem more real, was infinitely more terrible. Everything stood still for a second, as a panorama painted with three colours——the white of the smoke, the red of the shrapnel and blood, the green of the grass.

If I had felt nervous before, I did not feel so now, or at any rate not in anything like the same degree. As I advanced, I felt as if I was in a dream, but I had all my wits about me. We had been told to walk. Our boys, however, rushed forward with splendid impetuosity to help their comrades and smash the German resistance in the front line. What happened to our materials for blocking the German communication trench, when we got to our objective, I should not like to think. I kept up a fast walking pace and tried to keep the line together. This was impossible. When we had jumped clear of the remains of our front line trench, my platoon slowly disappeared through the line stretching out. For a long time, however, Sergeant S—— l, Lance-corporal M—— , Rifleman D—— , whom I remember being just in front of me, raising his hand in the air and cheering, and myself kept together.

Eventually Lance-corporal M—— was the only one of my platoon left near me, and I shouted out to him, "Let's try and keep together." It was not long, however, before we also parted company. One thing I remember very well about this time, and that was that a hare jumped up and rushed towards and past me through the dry, yellowish grass, its eyes bulging with fear.

We were dropping into a slight valley. The shell-holes were less few, but bodies lay all over the ground, and a terrible groaning arose from all sides. At one time we seemed to be advancing in little groups. I was at the head of one for a moment or two, only to realise shortly afterwards that I was alone.

I came up to the German wire. Here one could hear men shouting to one another and the wounded groaning above the explosions of shells and bombs and the rattle of machine-guns. I found myself with J—— , an officer of "C" company, afterwards killed while charging a machine-gun in the open. We looked round to see what our fourth line was doing. My company's fourth line had no leader. Captain W—— k, wounded twice, had fallen into a shell-hole, while Sergeant S—— r had been killed during the preliminary bombardment. Men were kneeling and firing. I started back to see if I could bring them up, but they were too far away. I made a cup of my mouth and shouted, as J—— was shouting. We could not be heard. I turned round again and advanced to a gap in the German wire. There was a pile of our wounded here on the German parapet.

Suddenly I cursed. I had been scalded in the left hip. A shell, I thought, had blown up in a water-logged crump-hole and sprayed me with boiling water. Letting go of my rifle, I dropped forward full length on the ground. My hip began to smart unpleasantly, and I left a curious warmth stealing down my left leg. I thought it was the boiling water that had scalded me. Certainly my breeches looked as if they were saturated with water. I did not know that they were saturated with blood.

So I lay, waiting with the thought that I might recover my strength (I could barely move) and try to crawl back. There was the greater possibility of death, but there was also the possibility of life. I looked around to see what was happening. In front lay some wounded; on either side of them stakes and shreds of barbed wire twisted into weird contortions by the explosions of our trench-mortar bombs. Beyond this nothing but smoke, interspersed with the red of bursting bombs and shrapnel.

From out this ghastly chaos crawled a familiar figure. It was that of Sergeant K—— , bleeding from a wound in the chest. He came crawling towards me.

"Hallo, K—— ," I shouted.

"Are you hit, sir?" he asked.

"Yes, old chap, I am," I replied.

"You had better try and crawl back," he suggested.

"I don't think I can move," I said.

"I'll take off your equipment for you."

He proceeded very gallantly to do this. I could not get to a kneeling position myself, and he had to get hold of me, and bring me to a kneeling position, before undoing my belt and shoulder-straps. We turned round and started crawling back together. I crawled very slowly at first. Little holes opened in the ground on either side of me, and I understood that I was under the fire of a machine-gun. In front bullets were hitting the turf and throwing it four or five feet into the air. Slowly but steadily I crawled on. Sergeant K—— and I lost sight of one another. I think that he crawled off to the right and I to the left of a mass of barbed wire entanglements.

I was now confronted by a danger from our own side. I saw a row of several men kneeling on the ground and firing. It is probable that they were trying to pick off German machine-gunners, but it seemed very much as if they would "pot" a few of the returning wounded into the bargain.

"For God's sake, stop firing," I shouted.

Words were of no avail. I crawled through them. At last I got on my feet and stumbled blindly along.

I fell down into a sunken road with several other wounded, and crawled up over the bank on the other side. The Germans had a ma-chine-gun on that road, and only a few of us got across. Someone faintly called my name behind me. Looking round, I thought I recognised a man of "C" company. Only a few days later did it come home to me that he was my platoon observer. I had told him to stay with me whatever happened. He had carried out his orders much more faithfully than I had ever meant, for he had come to my assistance, wounded twice in the head himself. He hastened forward to me, but, as I looked round waiting, uncertain quite as to who he was, his rifle clattered on to the ground, and he crumpled up and fell motionless just behind me. I felt that there was nothing to be done for him. He died a hero, just as he had always been in the trenches, full of self-control, never complaining, a ready volunteer. Shortly afterwards I sighted the remains of our front line trench and fell into them.

At first I could not make certain as to my whereabouts. Coupled with the fact that my notions in general were becoming somewhat hazy, the trenches themselves were entirely unrecognisable. They were filled with earth, and about half their original depth. I decided, with that quick, almost semi-conscious intuition that comes to one in moments of peril, to proceed to the left (to one coming from the German lines). As I crawled through holes and over mounds I could hear the vicious spitting of machine-gun bullets. They seemed to skim just over my helmet.

The trench, opening out a little, began to assume its old outline. I had reached the head of New Woman Street, though at the time I did not know what communication trench it was——or trouble, for that matter. The scene at the head of that communication trench is stamped in a blurred but unforgettable way on my mind. In the remains of a wrecked dug-out or emplacement a signaller sat, calmly transmitting messages to Battalion Headquarters. A few bombers were walking along the continuation of the front line. I could distinguish the red grenades on their arms through the smoke. There were more of them at the head of the communication trench. Shells were coming over and blowing up round about.

I asked one of the bombers to see what was wrong with my hip. He started to get out my iodine tube and field dressing. The iodine tube was smashed. I remembered that I had a second one, and we managed to get that out after some time. Shells were coming over so incessantly and close that the bomber advised that we should walk farther down the trench before commencing operations. This done, he opened my breeches and disclosed a small hole in the front of the left hip. It was bleeding fairly freely. He poured in the iodine, and put the bandage round in the best manner possible. We set off down the communication trench again, in company with several bombers, I holding the bandage to my wound.

We scrambled up mounds and jumped over craters (rather a painful performance for one wounded in the leg); we halted at times in almost open places, when machine-gun bullets swept unpleasantly near, and one felt the wind of shells as they passed just over, blowing up a few yards away. In my last stages across No Man's Land my chief thought had been, "I must get home now for the sake of my people." Now, for I still remember it distinctly, my thought was, "Will my name appear in the casualty list under the head of 'Killed' or 'Wounded'?" and I summoned up a mental picture of the two alternatives in black type.

After many escapes we reached the Reserve Line, where a military policeman stood at the head of Woman Street. He held up the men in front of me and directed them to different places. Someone told him that a wounded officer was following. This was, perhaps, as well, for I was an indistinguishable mass of filth and gore. My helmet was covered with mud, my tunic was cut about with shrapnel and bullets and saturated with blood; my breeches had changed from a khaki to a purple hue; my puttees were in tatters; my boots looked like a pair of very muddy clogs.

The military policeman consigned me to the care of some excellent fellow, of what regiment I cannot remember. After walking, or rather stumbling, a short way down Woman Street, my guide and I came upon a gunner Colonel standing outside his dugout and trying to watch the progress of the battle through his field-glasses.

"Good-morning," he said.

"Good-morning, sir," I replied.

This opening of our little conversation was not meant to be in the least ironical, I can assure you. It seemed quite natural at the time.

"Where are you hit?" he asked.

"In the thigh, sir. I don't think it's anything very bad."

"Good. How are we getting on?"

"Well, I really can't say much for certain, sir. But I got nearly to their front line."

Walking was now becoming exceedingly painful and we proceeded slowly. I choked the groans that would rise to my lips and felt a cold perspiration pouring freely from my face. It was easier to get along by taking hold of the sides of the trench with my hands than by being supported by my guide. A party of bombers or carriers of some description passed us. We stood on one side to let them go by. In those few seconds my wound became decidedly stiffer, and I wondered if I would ever reach the end of the trenches on foot. At length the communication trench passed through a belt of trees, and we found ourselves in Cross Street.

Here was a First Aid Post, and R.A.M.C. men were hard at work. I had known those trenches for a month past, and I had never thought that Cross Street could appear so homelike. Hardly a shell was falling and the immediate din of battle had subsided. The sun was becoming hot, but the trees threw refreshing shadows over the wide, shallow brick-floored trenches built by the French two years before. The R.A.M.C. orderlies were speaking pleasant words, and men not too badly wounded were chatting gaily. I noticed a dresser at work on a man nearby, and was pleased to find that the man whose wounds were being attended to was my servant L——. His wound was in the hip, a nasty hole drilled by a machine-gun bullet at close quarters. He showed me his water-bottle, penetrated by another bullet, which had inflicted a further, but slight, wound.

There were many more serious cases than mine to be attended to. After about five or ten minutes an orderly slit up my breeches.

"The wound's in the front of the hip," I said.

"Yes, but there's a larger wound where the bullets come out, sir."

I looked and saw a gaping hole two inches in diameter.

"I think that's a Blighty one, isn't it?" I remarked.

"I should just think so, sir!" he replied.

"Thank God! At last!" I murmured vehemently, conjuring up visions of the good old homeland.

The orderly painted the iodine round both wounds and put on a larger bandage. At this moment R——, an officer of "D" company, came limping into Cross Street.

"Hallo, L——," he exclaimed, "we had better try and get down to hospital together."

We started in a cavalcade to walk down the remaining trenches into the village, not before my servant, who had insisted on staying with me, had remarked——

"I think I should like to go up again now, sir," and to which proposal I had answered very emphatically—

"You won't do anything of the sort, my friend!"

R—— led the way, with a man to help him, next came my servant, then two orderlies carrying a stretcher with a terribly wounded

Scottish private on it; another orderly and myself brought up the rear—and a very slow one at that!

Turning a corner, we found ourselves amidst troops of the battalion in reserve to us, all of them eager for news. A subaltern, with whom I had been at a Divisional School, asked how far we had got. I told him that we were probably in their second line by now. This statement caused disappointment. Every one appeared to believe that we had taken the three lines in about ten minutes. I must confess that the night before the attack I had entertained hopes that it would not take us much longer than this. As a matter of fact my battalion, or the remains of it, after three hours of splendid and severe fighting, managed to penetrate into the third line trench.

Loss of blood was beginning to tell, and my progress was getting slower every minute. Each man, as I passed, put his arm forward to help me along and said a cheery word of some kind or other. Down the wide, brick-floored trench we went, past shattered trees and battered cottages, through the rank grass and luxuriant wild flowers, through the rich, unwarlike aroma of the orchard, till we emerged into the village "boulevard."

The orderly held me under the arms till I was put on a wheeled stretcher and hurried along, past the "boulevard pool" with its surrounding elms and willows, and, at the end of the "boulevard," up a street to the left. A short way up this street on the right stood the Advanced Dressing Station——a well-sandbagged house reached through the usual archway and courtyard. A dugout, supplied with electric light and with an entrance of remarkable sandbag construction, had been tunnelled out beneath the courtyard. This was being used for operations.

In front of the archway and in the road stood two *padrés* directing the continuous flow of stretchers and walking wounded. They appeared to be doing all the work of organisation, while the R.A.M.C. doctors and surgeons had their hands full with dressings and operations. These were the kind of directions:

"Wounded Sergeant? Right. Abdominal wound? All right. Lift him off—gently now. Take him through the archway into the dugout."

"Dead? Yes! Poor fellow, take him down to the Cemetery."

"German? Dugout No. 2, at the end of the road on the right."

Under the superintendence of the R.C. "*padré*, a man whose sympathy and kindness I shall never forget, my stretcher was lifted off the carrier and I was placed in the archway. The *padré* loosened my bandage and looked at the wound, when he drew in his breath and asked if I was in much pain.

"Not an enormous amount," I answered, but asked for something to drink.

"Are you quite sure it hasn't touched the stomach?" he questioned, looking shrewdly at me.

I emphatically denied that it had, and he brought a blood-stained mug with a little tea at the bottom of it. I can honestly say that I never enjoyed a drink so much as that one.

Shells, high explosives and shrapnel, were coming over every now and then. I kept my helmet well over my head. This also served as a shade from the sun, for it was now about ten o'clock and a sultry day. I was able to obtain a view of events round about fairly easily. From time to time orderlies tramped through the archway, bearing stretcher-cases to the dugout. Another officer had been brought in and placed on the opposite side of the archway. The poor fellow, about nineteen, was more or less unconscious. His head and both hands were covered in bandages crimson with blood. So coated was he with mud and gore that I did not at first recognise him as an officer.

At the farther end of the arch a young private of about eighteen was lying on his side, groaning in the agony of a stomach wound and crying "Mother." The sympathetic *padré* did the best he could to comfort him. Out in the road the R.A.M.C. were dressing and bandaging the ever-increasing flow of wounded. Amongst them a captive German R.A.M.C. man, in green uniform, with a Red Cross round his sleeve, was visible, hard at work. Everything seemed so different from the deadly strife a thousand or so yards away. There, foe was inflicting wounds on foe; here were our men attending to the German wounded and the Germans attending to ours. Both sides were working so hard now to save life. There was a human touch about that scene in the ruined village street which filled one with a sense of mingled sadness and pleasure. Here were both sides united in a common attempt to repair the ravages of war. Humanity had at last asserted itself.

It was about eleven o'clock, I suppose, when the *padré* came up again to my stretcher and asked me if I should like to get on, as there was a berth vacant in an ambulance. The stretcher was hoisted up and slid into the bottom berth of the car. The berth above was occupied by an unconscious man. On the other side of the ambulance were four sitting cases—a private, a sergeant, a corporal, and a rifleman, the last almost unconscious. Those of us who could talk were very pleased with life, and I remember saying: "Thank God, we're out of that hell, boys!"

"What's wrong with him?" I asked the corporal, signifying the unconscious man.

"Hit in the lungs, sir. They've set him up on purpose."

The corporal, pulling out his cigarette case, offered cigarettes all round, and we started to smoke. The last scene that I saw in Hébuterne was that of three men dressing a tall badly wounded Prussian officer lying on the side of the road. The ambulance turned the corner out of the village. There followed three "crashes" and dust flew on to the floor of the car.

"Whizz-bangs," was the corporal's laconical remark.

We had passed the German road barrage, and were on our way to peace and safety.

CHAPTER 4

Toll of Attack

We climbed the little white road which led through the battery positions now almost silent, topped the crest, and dipped into Sailly-au-Bois. The village had been very little shelled since the night before, and appeared the same as ever, except that the intense traffic, which had flowed into it for the past month, had ceased. Limbers and lorries had done their work, and the only objects which filled the shell-scarred streets were slow-moving ambulances, little blood-stained groups of "walking wounded," and the troops of a new division moving up into the line.

Though we were all in some pain as the ambulance jolted along through the ruts in the side of the road, we felt rather sorry for those poor chaps as they peered inside the car. Our fate was decided, theirs still hung in the balance. How often on the march one had looked back oneself into a passing ambulance and wished, rather shamefully, for a "Blighty" one. Sunburnt and healthy they looked as they shouted after us: "Good luck, boys, give our love to Blighty."

At the end of the village the ambulance swung off on a road leading to the left. It must have crossed the track by which my platoon and I had gone up the night before. About 11.30 a.m. we arrived at Couin, the headquarters of the First Field Ambulance.

A hum of conversation and joking arose from every side, and, with some exceptions, you could not have found such a cheery gathering anywhere. The immediate strain of battle had passed, and friends meeting friends compared notes of their experiences in the "show." Here a man with a bandaged arm was talking affectionately to a less fortunate "pal" on a stretcher, and asking him if he could do anything for him; it is extraordinary how suffering knits men together, and how much sympathy is brought out in a man at the sight of a badly wounded comrade: yonder by the huts an orderly assisted a "walking case," shot through the lungs and vomiting blood freely.

Nearby I recognised E—— 's servant of the L—— S—— . When he had finished giving some tea or water to a friend, I hailed him and asked him if Mr. E—— was hit. Mr. E—— , he told me, had been laid up for some days past, and had not taken part in the attack. He was, however, going round and writing letters for the men. Would I like to see him? We were fairly good acquaintances, so I said that I should. Presently he arrived.

"Bad luck, old chap. Where have you caught it?" he asked.

"In the thigh," I replied.

He wrote two postcards home for me, one home and another to relatives, and I did my best to sign them. I remember that on one of them was inscribed: "This is to let you know that E—— has been caught bending," and wondering what my grandfather, a doctor, would make out of that!

The sun was beating down on us now, and since, after I had been duly labelled "G.S.W. (gun-shot wound) Back," a Medical Staff Officer advised that I should be transferred into the officers' hut, I entered its cooler shades with much gladness.

Captain W—— t came in soon afterwards. In the second line German trench he had looked over the *parados* to see if any opposition was coming up from the third line trench, and had been hit by a machine-gun bullet in the shoulder. In making his way home he had been hit twice again in the shoulder. H—— also put in an appearance with a bullet wound in the arm. He had taken a party of "walking wounded" up to Sailly-au-Bois, and got a car on. A doctor brought round the familiar old beverage of tea, which in large quantities, and in company with whisky, had helped us through many an unpleasant day in the trenches. Captain W—— t refused it, and insisted on having some bread and jam. I took both with much relish, and, having appeased an unusually large appetite, got an orderly to wash my face and hands, which were coated with blood.

"I dare say you feel as you was gettin' back to civilisation again, sir," he said. Much refreshed, and quietly looking at a new number of *The Tatler*, I certainly felt as if I was, though, in spite of an air ring, the wound was feeling rather uncomfortable. At the end of the hut two or three poor fellows were dying of stomach wounds. It was a peculiar contrast to hear two or three men chatting gaily just outside my end of the hut. I could only catch fragments of the conversation, which I give here.

"When Mr. A—— gave the order to advance, I went over like a bird."

"The effect of the rum, laddie!"

"Mr A—— was going strong too."

"What's happened to Mr. A——, do you know?"

"Don't know. I didn't see 'im after that."

"'E's all right. Saw him just now. Got a wound in the arm."

"Good. Isn't the sun fine here? Couldn't want a better morning for an attack, could you?"

The hut was filling rapidly, and the three stomach cases being quite hopeless were removed outside. A doctor brought in an officer of the K—— 's. He was quite dazed, and sank full length on a bed, passing his hand across his face and moaning. He was not wounded, but had been blown up whilst engaged in cutting a communication trench across No Man's Land, they told me. It was not long, however, before he recovered his senses sufficiently enough to walk with help to an ambulance. A *padré* entered, supporting a young officer of the ——, a far worse case of shell shock, and laid him out on the bed. He had no control over himself, and was weeping hysterically.

"For God's sake don't let me go back, don't send me back!" he cried.

The *padré* tried to comfort him.

"You'll soon be in a nice hospital at the Base, old chap, or probably in England."

He looked at the *padré* blankly, not understanding a word that he was saying.

A more extraordinary case of shell shock was that of an officer lying about three beds down from me. In the usual course of events an R.A.M.C. corporal asked him his name.

"F—— ," he replied in a vague tone.

The corporal thought that he had better make certain, so with as polite a manner as possible looked at his identification disc.

"It puts Lt. B—— here," he said.

There followed a lengthy argument, at the end of which the patient said——

"Well, it's no use. You had better give it up. I don't know what my name is!"

A Fusilier officer was carried in on a stretcher and laid next to me. After a time he said—

"Is your name L—— ?"

I replied affirmatively.

"Don't you recognise me?" he questioned.

I looked at him, but could not think where I had seen him before.

"My name's D—— . I was your Company Quartermaster-Sergeant in the Second Battalion." Then I remembered him, though it had been hard to recognise him in officer's uniform, blood-stained and tattered at that. We compared notes of our experiences since I had left the second line of my battalion in England nearly a year before, until, soon afterwards, he was taken out to an ambulance.

At the other end of the hut it was just possible to see an officer tossing to and fro deliriously on a stretcher. I use the word "deliriously," though he was probably another case of shell shock. He was wounded also, judging by the bandages which swathed the middle part of his body. The poor fellow thought that he was still fighting, and every now and again broke out like this—

"Keep 'em off, boys. Keep 'em off. Give me a bomb, sergeant. Get down! My God! I'm hit. Put some more of those sandbags on the barricade. These damned shells! Can I stand it any longer? Come on, boys. Come along, sergeant! We must go for them. Oh! my God! I must stick it!"

After a time the cries became fainter, and the stretcher was taken out.

About three o'clock I managed to get a doctor to inject me with anti-tetanus. I confess that I was rather anxious about getting this done, for in crawling back across No Man's Land my wound had been covered with mud and dirt. The orderly, who put on the iodine, told me that the German artillery was sending shrapnel over the ridge. This was rather disconcerting, but, accustomed as I had become to shrapnel at close quarters, the sounds seemed so distant that I did not bother more about them.

It must have been about four o'clock when my stretcher was picked up and I passed once again into the warm sunlight. Outside an orderly relieved me of my steel and gas helmets, in much the same way as the collector takes your ticket when you pass through the gates of a London terminus in a taxi. Once more the stretcher was slid into an ambulance, and I found myself in company with a young subaltern of the K—— 's. He was very cheery, and continued to assert that we should all be in "Blighty" in a day or two's time. When the

A.S.C. driver appeared at the entrance of the car and confirmed our friend's opinion, I began to entertain the most glorious visions of the morrow—visions which I need hardly say did not come true.

"How were you hit?" I asked the officer of the K——'s.

"I got a machine-gun bullet in the pit of the stomach while digging that communication trench into No Man's Land. It's been pretty bad, but the pain's going now, and I think I shall be all right."

Then he recognised the man on the stretcher above me.

"Hullo, laddie," he said. "What have they done to you?"

"I've been hit in the left wrist and the leg, sir. I hope you aren't very bad."

The engine started, and we set off on our journey to the Casualty Clearing Station. For the last time we passed the villages, which we had come to know so intimately in the past two months during rest from the trenches. There was Souastre, where one had spent pleasant evenings at the Divisional Theatre; St. Amand with its open square in front of the church, the meeting-place of the villagers, now deserted save for two or three soldiers; Gaudiempré, the headquarters of an Army Service Corps park, with its lines of roughly made stables. At one part of the journey a 15-inch gun let fly just over the road. We had endured quite enough noise for that day, and I was glad that it did not occur again. From a rather tortuous course through bye-lanes we turned into the main Arras to Doullens road—that long, straight, typical French highway with its avenue of poplars. Shortly afterwards the ambulance drew up outside the Casualty Clearing Station.

The Casualty Clearing Station was situated in the grounds of a *château*. I believe that the *château* itself was used as a hospital for those cases which were too bad to be moved farther. We were taken into a long cement-floored building, and laid down in a line of stretchers which ran almost from the doorway up to a screen at the end of the room, behind which dressings and operations were taking place. On my right was the officer of the K——'s, still fairly cheery, though in a certain amount of pain; on my left lay a rifleman hit in the chest, and very grey about the face; I remember that, as I looked at him, I compared the colour of his face with that of the stomach cases I had seen. A stomach case, as far as I can remember, has an ashen pallor about the face; a lung case has a haggard grey look.

Next to him a boy of about eighteen was sitting on his stretcher; he was hit in the jaw, the arms, and the hands, but he calmly took out his pipe, placed it in his blood-stained mouth, and started smoking. I was talking to the officer of the K——'s, when he suddenly fell to groaning, and rolled over on to my stretcher. I tried to comfort him, but words were of no avail. A doctor came along, asked a few questions, and examined the wound, just a small hole in the pit of the stomach; but he looked serious enough about it. The stretcher was lifted up and its tortured occupant borne away behind the screen for an operation. That was the last I saw of a very plucky young fellow. I ate some bread and jam, and drank some tea doled out liberally all down the two lines of stretchers, for another line had formed by now.

My turn came at last, and I was carried off to a table behind the screen, where the wound was probed, dressed, and bandaged tightly, and I had a foretaste of the less pleasant side of hospital life. There were two Army nurses at work on a case next to mine—the first English women I had seen since I returned from leave six months before. My wound having been dressed, I was almost immediately taken out and put into a motor-lorry. There must have been about nine of us, three rows of three, on the floor of that lorry. I did not find it comfortable, though the best had been done under the circumstances to make it so; neither did the others, many of whom were worse wounded than myself, judging by the groans which arose at every jolt.

We turned down a road leading to the station. Groups of peasants were standing in the village street and crying after us: "Ah! *les pauvres blessés! les pauvres Anglais blessés!*" These were the last words of gratitude and sympathy that the kind peasants could give us. We drew up behind other cars alongside the hospital train, and the engine-driver looked round from polishing his engine and watched us with the wistful gaze of one to whom hospital train work was no longer a novelty. Walking wounded came dribbling up by ones and twos into the station yard, and were directed into sitting compartments.

The sun was in my eyes, and I felt as if my face was being scorched. I asked an R.A.M.C.N.C.O., standing at the end of the wagon, to get me something to shade my eyes. Then occurred what I felt was an extremely thoughtful act on the part of a wounded man. A badly wounded lance-corporal, on the other side of the lorry, took out his handkerchief and stretched it over to me. When I asked him if he was sure that he did not want it, he insisted on my taking it. It was dirty and blood-stained, but saved me much discomfort, and I thanked him profusely. After about ten minutes our stretchers were hauled out of the lorry. I was borne up to the officers' carriage at the far end of the train. It was a splendidly equipped compartment; and when I found myself between the sheets of my berth, with plenty of pillows under me, I felt as if I had definitely got a stage nearer to England. Some one behind me called my name, and, looking round, I saw my old friend M—— W——, whose party I had nearly run into the night before in that never-to-be-forgotten communication trench, Woman Street. He told me that he had been hit in the wrist and leg. Judging by his flushed appearance, he had something of a temperature.

More wounded were brought or helped in—men as well as officers——till the white walls of the carriage were lined with blood-stained, mud-covered khaki figures, lying, sitting, and propped up in various positions.

The Medical Officer in charge of the train came round and asked us what we should like to drink for dinner.

"Would you like whisky-and-soda, or beer, or lemonade?" he questioned me. This sounded pleasant to my ears, but I only asked for a lemonade.

As the train drew out of the station, one caught a last glimpse of warfare——an aeroplane, wheeling round in the evening sky amongst a swarm of tell-tale smoke-puffs, the explosions of "Archie" shells.

One Young Man

John Ernest Hodder-Williams

Contents

To the Greatly Beloved Memory
Of
One Young Man
Who Founded the Y.M.C.A.
My Uncle
Sir George Williams

Foreword

I am glad that this very personal little book is to be republished, if only for private circulation, for it rings as true today as it did yesterday.

It tells the story of one young man in the Great War, but, in fact, it reveals no less the personality of the writer who knit the young man's story together.

The young man continues—the writer has passed on.

My brother is revealed here, not as the famous publisher, but as a man whose sympathy was so quick and passionate that he literally lived the suffering and trials of others.

It is this living sympathy, given so freely, that lies like a wreath of everlasting flowers on his memory now.

It is no longer a secret that the real name of the "Sydney Baxter" of this story is Reginald Davis; and those of us who know him and have watched every step of his progress, from his first small job of the "pen and ledger" to the Secretaryship of a great Company, are astonished at the understanding and accuracy of this portrayal of a young man's inner self and outer deeds.

It is true that Sir Ernest Hodder-Williams did little more than comment on the diary written by Davis himself. But how well he explains it; how well he reads into its touching cheerfulness and its splendid sorrow the eternal truth that only by suffering and obedience can the purposes of God and man be fulfilled.

Davis has won his spurs. He bears the marks of his service in the Great War with honour and with never a complaint. His old chief and chronicler was proud of him then. He would be proud of him today.

R. Percy Hodder-Williams.

CHAPTER 1

Introduces One Young Man

The boys in the office were, I fancy, a bit prejudiced against him before he arrived. It wasn't his fault, for he was a stranger to them all, but it got about that the dear old "chief" had decided to engage a real good Sunday-school boy. Someone had heard him say, or, more likely, thought it would be funny to imagine him saying, that the advent of such a boy might "improve the general tone" of the place. That, you'll admit, was pretty rough on Sydney Baxter—the boy in question. Now Sydney Baxter is not his real name, but this I can vouch is his true story. For the most part it is told exactly in his own words. You'll admit its truth when you have read it, for there isn't a line in it which will stretch your imagination a hair's breadth. It's the plain unvarnished tale of an average young man who joined the army because he considered it his duty—who fought for many months. That's why I am trying to record it; for if I tell it truly I shall have written the story of many thousands—I shall have written a page of the nation's history.

And so I need not warn you at the beginning that this book does *not* end with a V.C. and cheering throngs. It may possibly end with wedding bells, but you will agree there's nothing out of the common about that—and a good job too.

I think on the whole I will keep Sydney Baxter's real name to myself. For one thing he is still in the army; for another he is expected back at the same office when he is discharged from hospital. It's rather beginning at the wrong end to mention the hospital at this stage, but, as I've done so, I'd better explain that after going unscathed through Ypres and Hill 60, and all the trench warfare that followed, Sydney Baxter was wounded in nine places at the first battle of the Somme on that ever-glorious and terrible first of July. He is, as I write, waiting for a glass eye; he has a silver plate where part of his frontal bone used to be; is minus one whole finger, and the best part of a second. He is deep scarred from his eyelid to his hair. I can tell you he looks as if he had been through it. Well, he has.

He was nicknamed "Gig-lamps" in the office. He wore large spectacles and his face was unhealthily lacking in traces of the open air. He was in demeanour a very typical son of religious parents—well brought up, shielded, shepherded, a little spoiled, a little soft perhaps, and maybe a trifle self-consciously righteous. A good boy, a home boy. No need for me to pile on the adjectives—you know exactly the kind of chap he was. One more thing, however, and very important—he had a sense of humour and he was uniformly good tempered and willing. That is why, in a short time, the prejudice of the office gave way to open approval. "Young Baxter may be a 'pi' youth, but he's quick at his job, and nothing's too much trouble for him," said his boss. And against their previous judgment the boys liked him. He could see a joke. He was a good sort.

Curiously enough it was the Y.M.C.A. that first introduced Sydney Baxter to what, for want of a better term, we will call the sporting side of life. There's a fine sporting side to every real Englishman's life—don't let there be any mistake about that. "He is a sportsman" is not, as a few excellent people seem to believe, a term of reproach. It is one of the highest honours conferred on an officer by the men he commands. And in the ranks "a good sport" is often another way of spelling "a hero."

It was, as I say, at the Y.M.C.A. that this one young man was first taken out of himself and his quiet home surroundings, first became interested in the convivialities of life. In those days, to be quite frank about it, a certain settled staidness of demeanour, a decided aloofness from the outside world, marked many religious households. A book of unexceptional moral tone, and probably containing what was known as "definite teaching," was the main relaxation after working hours—that, and an occasional meeting and some secretarial work for a religious or charitable society. Companions, if any, were very carefully chosen by the parents. Well, war has changed all that—it has even chosen our very bed-fellows for us. And no questions to be asked, either.

It is often assumed by those who know no better that such a home as Sydney Baxter's produces either prigs or profligates. As a matter of fact, one of the reasons of this book is to prove that out of such a home may come, I believe often does come, the best type of Englishman—a Christian sportsman, a man who fights all the better for his country because he has been taught from childhood to fear God and hate iniquity.

But it was well for Sydney Baxter that he prepared for the chances and quick changes of his military life by learning how to make the best of his hitherto hidden gift of companionship.

This is how it came about. He writes:

One afternoon in early autumn a card was put into the hands of every young man in our office, inviting us to a tea and social evening at the Y.M.C.A. Headquarters. The chaps said to me, 'Of course *you* are going, Baxter?' and I answered, 'Why not?' They, however, seemed to be of the opinion that the tea was, more or less, a bait to a prayer-meeting or something of that kind. However, several went, expecting, and preparing themselves for, the worst. We were welcomed by a group of gentlemen who seemed to be possessors of smiles of permanency; they conducted us to a large room already well filled with others like ourselves, whom we incorrectly judged to be members, as they seemed to be quite at home. In every corner of the room were lounge chairs and on the tables games of all description. Here and there small groups were being entertained by the members, and, judging by the unrestrained merriment, they were proving themselves very capable hosts.

We were told to make ourselves absolutely at home; and although we entered with zest into all that was going on, I don't think really that we quite lost the feeling that a prayer-meeting was bound to follow. Much to our surprise no one came up and spoke to us about our souls; indeed our hosts led the way into all the fun that was going, and none of them had the milk-and-bun expression of countenance that we had conjured up in our mind's eye. You can see what our conception of Y.M.C.A. members was. We imagined them a narrow-minded set of some mild kind of religious fanatics.

I promised a veracious chronicle, and I am quoting Sydney Baxter word for word. I am inclined to believe that here he is expressing his companions' anxieties rather than his own.

"The tea gong sounded and our hosts led the way to another large room, and upon the tables was a sumptuous spread. Being young men we did full justice to it, and throughout the whole of tea time this same atmosphere of sociability surrounded us.

After tea we were escorted to the lecture room, and, although it is too long ago to remember who the speakers were, and what the subjects, I do know it was most enjoyable. At the conclusion we were given a hearty welcome to come and use the rooms every evening for reading, writing, or social intercourse and games. The following morning in the office we all agreed that we had had a most enjoyable evening, and that we had badly misjudged the Y.M.C.A. A few of us took advantage of the invitation and went again, and received the same warm welcome and had another enjoyable evening. Shortly afterwards three of us joined the Association. Until this time I had no idea of the magnitude of the Association's work; my idea was that little existed outside of the Headquarters and the smaller branches over the country. This was some eight years ago. Now everyone knows the Y.M.C.A. I soon got into the stream and found I was in the midst of a large number of football, cricket, swimming, and rowing enthusiasts. The teams that the Association clubs put into the field and on the river were very strong. The sports side of the Y.M.C.A. was indeed a revelation.

So it was that Sydney Baxter's evenings and weekends were often spent with his fellows in various Y.M.C.A. organisations. He was anxious to get on, and the Association classes helped him, too, in his business education. Ambitious of advancement in the office, he had noted that his schooling was lacking in certain essentials if he was to be fit when the opportunity arrived. He rose quickly in the business and was soon doing responsible work. He was one of those fellows who get ready for the time when their chance may come. It always does come to such as Sydney Baxter.

The Association tackled the holiday problem for this young man too. This is how he describes his first visit to one of the Y.M.C.A. hotels. He calls them hotels himself, and I am not surprised, for such they really are. A "home," though a beautiful word, does not, somehow, in this connection convey the proper idea of these Y.M.C.A. holiday resorts. "*A home from home*"—well you know!

I went down entirely on my own. I was at that time a very reserved chap, and I had misgivings as to the probability of making chums. I shared my room with a young Frenchman, who fortunately could speak English quite well, and thus we were saved embarrassing silence and aloofness.

"Tea gong sounded, and as we made our way into the passage we were literally carried along in the stream of young men, newcomers in their lounge suits, the others mostly in flannels. On we swept, down the stairs into the large dining-hall. Sit where you please, act as if you had been here all your life and treat everyone as an old pal, seemed to be the order of the day, and in that atmosphere it was impossible to feel anything but quite at home. Before tea was over we new arrivals were infected with the same spirit of joviality, and were ready for the first 'rag.'

I was shown the house and grounds by an old boarder. In addition to the lounge, writing and smoking-rooms, there was a dark-room for developing, a fully rigged 'gym,' and billiard-room; and so, in inclement weather, every amusement was at hand. In the grounds were tennis courts and croquet lawns.

Every week drives were arranged to the beauty-spots and historical places round about, but I appreciated most the facilities offered by a temporary membership of the boating club for the absurdly small sum of 3s. 6d. per week. For this one could have a skiff or, if a party, a large boat, any day for any length of time, bathing costume and fishing tackle thrown in. I took full advantage of this, and most mornings and afternoons were spent on the water. We used to pull over to the obsolete battleships that lay in the stretch of water between us and the mainland. Here we would tether up and turn the gangway into a diving platform. Happy indeed were these days spent with companions who were in every sense of the word sportsmen and gentlemen.

Sportsmen and gentlemen—a new designation, perhaps, to some who have judged these Y.M.C.A. members by hearsay only. It's Sydney Baxter's not mine. And he ought to know well what the words mean after two years in a line regiment at the front.

CHAPTER 2

One Young Man Joins the Army

Sydney Baxter was most decidedly getting on in business. And then the war came. I do not want you to have the impression that, at this time, he was one of those sturdy, strapping young fellows who gladly rushed into the ranks for the very joy of fighting. There were thousands of them, I know, a glorious breed, but Sydney Baxter was not of that build. So that there may be no mistake let me give his own words. They are frank enough to be convincing.

When war fell upon Europe I was one of those foolish people who imagined that the *Kaiser* and his army would be completely crushed before Xmas, 1914. For the first two months I never gave a thought to the possibility of my becoming a soldier. I couldn't imagine myself with a rifle and bayonet chasing Huns, or standing the rough-and-ready life of the soldier, and the thought of blood was horrible. I had worn glasses since I was a boy of twelve, and for that reason, among others, I had not learnt the art of self-defence where quickness of vision is half the battle. From appearances and manners one would have ticketed me as a Conscientious Objector. I thank God I had not *that* conception of my duty to Him.

And so Sydney Baxter went on with his work. There was plenty to do. Reservists had been called up. Opportunities of advancement were many. Some must stay and "keep the home fires burning." You know all the arguments, all the self-justification of those days. His chance had undoubtedly arrived. He was badly needed in the office. You shall read his own confession.

It was well into October before I realised the Call to Arms was a personal one, and that the Hun was not so easily to be beaten.

The treatment of the Belgians hit me very hard, and, but for my home circumstances, I should have donned khaki straight away. My position was just this. My father had died some few months before, and left to my care my mother and my sister. Their protection was my solemn charge—there was no doubt about it in my mind. And yet, what was my duty? To fight—or to stay and look after our little home? It is a problem that thousands of us young men have had to wrestle with, and for several days I wrestled with it alone. Mother was purely neutral; she refused to influence me either way. Mother-like she could not encourage my going, but she would never lift a finger to deter me. Her answer was that it was entirely a matter of what *I* conscientiously felt was my foremost duty. I never went near a recruiting meeting, so that I should not be carried away by enthusiasm to the recruiting office. I must decide when my thoughts were cool and collected. The second week in November brought the climax. I knew my duty was to fight.

So I enlisted in a London Territorial Regiment whose first battalion was already in France and would require frequent drafts. I did not hesitate about joining a fighting unit. Other units are very necessary, but I wouldn't let another man do *my* fighting for me. I had some difficulty about a slightly weak heart caused by a severe illness a few years before. However, with the words that 'the life would either make or break me,' I was accepted for active service.

I am told that Sydney Baxter omits one thing here. Unlike so many in those early days, when he announced to the chief that he had joined, he asked no question about any possible allowance. He asked no advice, he suggested no help. He just joined. All he said was, "I felt I had to go, sir, and my mother says it will be all right. She says she will be able to manage quite well." Let me pay my tribute to this one young man's mother. There are so many like her that I pay it to thousands. Not only did she refuse to put obstacles in the way, but she would have no bargaining with patriotism. "She would manage quite well." It meant more boarders in the little home, it meant the breaking up of the old sweet privacy and quietude of the household, but—she would manage quite well. God knows the heartache and the sorrow behind the sacrifice she and the thousands like her have made—surely a sacrifice very acceptable in His sight.

CHAPTER 3

One Young Man in Camp

Within a fortnight this one young man was in camp at Crowborough. The contrast to his previous life as a city clerk, where mud was unknown and wet feet a rare occurrence, was marked indeed. The camp was sodden, the mud ankle-deep, and, what with that and the cold November weather, times were pretty stiff. He writes home:

Our camp is about a foot deep in mud and slosh, and every time you go out your boots are covered and you have to be careful or you slip over.

Our huts are like Church Missions. There are sixty-one fellows in this one, and all along the sides are our mattresses which we fold up. They are made of straw and are really very comfortable. The only drawback is that in the morning you find your toes sticking out at the other end of the bed. I must tell you how these beds are made. There are three planks about six feet in length, and these are placed side by side on two trestles about ten inches high. They give us three blankets, very thick and warm, and you can roll them round yourself.

Right down the centre of the room are long trestled tables with forms to sit on, and this is where we feast. We sleep, eat, drink, play games, write letters, and do everything in this room.

It's very funny to hear the bugle-calls. Everything is done by bugles. At 6.30 in the morning there is the first call and everyone gets up. If you don't—the sergeant comes along and pulls you out. To wash we have to run down to the other end of the camp and fill our buckets. There are only two buckets for sixty chaps, so you can imagine the scramble. For a bathroom we have a large field, and we nearly break our backs bending down over the basins. For about one hour before breakfast we do physical drill with our coats off. And hard work it is. For breakfast we have streaky greasy bacon. Funny—at home, I never ate bacon, I couldn't stick it, but here I walk into it and enjoy it. The tea they give us is not ideal, but so long as it is hot and wet it goes down all right. For dinner it's stew—stew—stew, but it's not bad. Of course, some day I get all gravy and no meat, another day meat and no gravy. Tea is quite all right. We have plenty of bread, butter, jam, and cheese. All food is fetched in dixeys (large boilers), and tea, stew, and bacon are all cooked in turn in these, so if the orderlies don't wash them clean at dinner time we have greasy, stewy tea.

I am getting a bit used to the marching, especially when there is anyone singing. The favourites are 'John Peel,' 'Cock Robin,' 'Oh, who will o'er the downs so free?' 'John Brown's Body,' 'Hearts of Oak,' and 'Annie Laurie.' We all have little books of Camp Songs, and we learn them at night; it makes all the difference to the marching. One of the songs is:—

Oh, Mother is the leader of society, and
You can see her name is in the papers every day.
She was presented at the court
For fighting Mrs. Short
Down our way.

Not an exactly edifying song, but it goes with a swing. I can hardly keep my eyes open as I write this.

On the whole and considering everything—a wide phrase covering many things unspoken—Sydney Baxter enjoyed his camp life, but Christmas was certainly a hardship. He writes:

Christmas Day, 1914.

All day yesterday I was on fatigue work, and did not finish until 7.30 to 8. We started the morning by building a hedge with bushes gathered from the Heath, and then we unloaded trucks of hay and straw and built them in a stack. I got several stray pieces down my neck. After that we had to unload a traction load of coal in one-cwt. sacks, and oh, they were dirty and awkward too. We had sacks over our heads like ordinary coalmen, and you ought to have seen our hands and faces when we had finished. We could not get any tea, as we were expecting three more trolleys. After about two hours the trolleys came, and we unloaded some meat; it took three of us to lift some of the pieces. Then after that bacon, oats, tea, jam, and about 1,000 loaves of bread. We were proper Jacks-of-all-trades and were thoroughly tired out.

This seems a funny sort of Christmas Day, but it will be all right after five o'clock. Of course I'd rather be in London and see you all. Still, all the same I'm rather enjoying myself this afternoon. I have a big box of chocs. by the side of me, and they are gradually diminishing. And now I feel in a better mood."

The Y.M., as it is now always called by the men at and from the front, played a very important part, an invaluable part, in Sydney Baxter's camp life. He writes:

We were about twenty minutes' walk from the village, and at first there was absolutely nothing there to go down for, and we seemed doomed to a very uncomfortable winter. However, the words of a well-known war song, 'Every cloud is silver lined,' are very true. *Our* cloud was soon brightly lined by the Y.M. people, who discovered the best way to do it in no time. A hall was acquired in the village for the sale of tea and eatables, and for facilitating writing and reading for the troops in camp. It was staffed by ladies in the locality and was a real Godsend to us all. Picture us from 6.30 a.m. to 4 p.m. on and off parade, in a muddy camp, without even a semblance of a canteen or writing-hut, always within sound of the bugle with its ever-recurring call for Orderly Sergeants, tired out and wet through and inwardly chafing at the unaccustomed discipline. Our spirits were on a par with Bairnsfather's 'Fed-up one.' At the last note of 'the Retreat' we were free. Without the Y.M. touch we should have had to stay in our bleak huts, constantly reminded of our surroundings and discomforts. But these Y.M. people had provided a comfortable, well-lighted, and, above all, warm room, with plenty of books and papers and any amount of grub and unlimited tea to wash it down. Isn't it wonderful how many sorrows the British army can drown in a cup of tea?

Apparently there's no need to tell the Y.M. people to 'get a move on,' for before two months had elapsed they installed in the very centre of the camp a large canteen, with a reading and writing room. It made a big difference to us, as we had the advantage of procuring a midday cup of tea, coffee, or cocoa, and such luxuries as biscuits and chocolate, also an evening's enjoyment, without the weary trudge to and from the village. As the vaccinations and inoculations were in progress at that time, the warm room was a blessing and eased the wearisome day which would have had to be spent in camp. More and more huts were erected, and more and more men occupied them; so a very large new Y.M. hut was quickly built near the camps and was opened in state, some fifty of us forming a Guard of Honour. It was a splendid building—its greatest attraction the billiard tables. Night after night we waited our turn for a game. At the long counter were a library and post office; the latter was most useful, for a letter could be written and posted without any delay whatever. Refreshments were, as usual, obtained at any time. There was not the slightest fuss; anyone could enter and do exactly as he wished. There is a genuine Y.M. atmosphere which makes a fellow feel 'at home.' It says, 'We are here because we feel we are "kind of wanted" here for your individual comfort: this is *your show*, and we are happy and anxious to do all we can for you. Come at any time and bring all your chums.'

Sydney Baxter's chief saw him once or twice during these camp days. And he marvelled. The spectacles had gone. The lank, round-shouldered figure had filled and straightened. Suddenly a man had been born. A soldier, too. This fellow of the pen and ledger, this very type of the British clerk who had never handled a rifle in his life and didn't know the smell of powder from eau de Cologne, who had never experienced anything of hardship or even discomfort; whose outlook in life had hitherto never stretched beyond a higher seat at the office desk, to whom the great passions of life were a sealed book—this fellow passed his shooting and other tests in record time.

He was in France within sixteen weeks of joining the army.

Those were very dark days in England, but the sight of this one young man cheered the chief. We were arrayed in battle against men who had been trained through all the years of their manhood, the whole course of whose lives had been shaped for this Day. And we had to meet them with—clerks! It seemed hopeless and a mockery. But when he saw Sydney Baxter the chief realised that often when the spirit is willing the flesh becomes strong; that the British fighting breed was not dead, though the black office coat had misled the German. How many times have you and I said "he was the last man I should have thought would have made a soldier."

Well, Sydney Baxter was that last man. And he made a first-class soldier. Let this country never forget it. He, and the thousands like him, outnumbered and outgunned, fought the Prussian Guard, the most finished product of the German military machine, and halted them, held them, beat them. In equal fight they thrashed them. Think of it in the light of history. The greatest and most wonderfully equipped and trained army the world has ever known beaten in fair fight by an army of clerks, schoolmasters, stockbrokers, University men, street waifs, shopkeepers, labourers, counter-jumpers, most of whom did not know one end of a rifle from the other when war was declared. Sydney Baxter was one of that army. That is why I am telling his story. It will make strange and very salutary reading for Prussian arrogance—some day.

CHAPTER 4

One Young Man on Active Service

Sydney Baxter was sent with his unit to Rouen. He writes:

We were tightly packed in a small tent at Rouen Camp. The following morning and afternoon we were busily engaged in being fitted out with extra equipment and ammunition, and so did not have time to look around. We had great hopes, however, of seeing the city in the evening, but we had to 'Stand by' and on no account leave camp. This was horrible. The tents were too dark to play cards, we had no reading matter or letters to answer, and once more seemed doomed to an evening of deadly dreariness.

However, we decided to patrol the camp, my chum and I. As we walked off together we little dreamed that exactly one month from that day he was to be called upon to pay the supreme sacrifice of all. We walked round that camp, feeling that in each other we had our only link with home, with past associations. We did not speak much. Each had his own thoughts, each was subconsciously leaning on the other for support, for the coming unknown experiences. It was a cold March evening, and for want of anything to do, and in the hope of getting a little warmth, we decided to go back to our tent and turn in. I have tried to give an idea of how we were feeling; it can be summed up as tired and cold—and a bit homesick.

It was just then that we spotted a tent with the sign of 'The Red Triangle.' We had visions of hot tea. An oasis in the desert could not have been more welcome. We entered the large tent; it was very full, and a long line was patiently awaiting the turn for purchasing. There was no shouting, no pushing or elbowing to get up to the front and be served first. The tent was really and truly a haven of peace—such a welcome port of call. On the small tables were magazines and 'Blighty' newspapers, paper and envelopes were given for the asking, and a gramophone was grinding out the tunes we all loved. We sat at one of the tables, so thankful for such a change of scene, and for the warmth of the hot tea. The same welcome, the same homely atmosphere, were here as in the other Y.M. centres. One felt, *one was made to feel*, that his was the right to enter and stay and enjoy himself each in his own way, and that is why the Y.M. is so popular, and why both the taciturn and the jocular find their way by common consent to these Y.M.C.A. tents.

In a few days came the order to proceed to Ypres. He writes:

We swung round into the station yard, and were allotted to our compartments, fondly imagining we should be off in a few minutes. We took off our equipment and other paraphernalia, and settled down for our journey. A minute or so afterwards the order was passed down that the train would not start before 7 o'clock, and that men might leave their compartments but not the station. Here was a fine lookout. It was only about 2 o'clock, and we had to look forward to at least five hours of weary waiting, without anything hot to drink and only bully and biscuits to eat.

It was not a pleasant prospect, you will agree, but apparently it was nothing out of the usual, for the 'Association of the Red Triangle' was ready and waiting for us, and had a large canteen, run entirely by ladies, on the station. Here we were able to provide for our journey, fill our water-bottles with tea and our haversacks with ham, rolls, and fruit. This was the best refreshment room I have been into, and it was our last glimpse of English ladies for many months. These ladies are doing a splendid and most self-sacrificing work, for their hours are long and their duties heavy. I wonder if it has ever occurred to them how much their presence meant to us boys? For many they were the last seen of the womanhood of our race.

I wonder too. Will any of those ladies read these lines? I hope so—I'd like them to know what their presence meant to just one of the boys they have been serving so well. They will have their reward. I should like them to have just one word of a Tommy's thanks now.

He continues:

In our little compartment of six two were killed within a month and one wounded; the other three survived until the first of July, when one was killed, one was taken a prisoner of war, and I was wounded and rendered unfit for further service. When at last our train started, amid rousing cheers for the ladies and a fluttering of white handkerchiefs from the little group on the station platform, we seemed to leave the last of civilisation behind.

Before midnight we were under shell-fire in the Infantry Barracks of Ypres.

He writes to his mother:

My word we *were* tired at the end of the journey. We are stationed in the military barracks of the city, and have had a chance of looking round the town. The buildings, especially the cathedral, are very much damaged. The only discomforts are the lack of food and the absence of money to buy it. Both G. and I landed here without a penny, but managed to borrow enough to buy a loaf. We know now what it is to be hungry; we have ¼ lb. of bread a day only, and no milk in the tea, so you can see that what you want you must buy, and it's terribly expensive here, 6*d*. for a loaf, etc. But we shall be paid in a day or so. The only things which are really necessary, and which we cannot get here, are candles and Oxo cubes. Although I don't want to be a burden to you, I should like you to send 1 lb. of candles and some cubes. The candles are used for boiling water or tea, etc., in the trenches, and it is the only way we can get anything hot. Of course anything in the way of food is acceptable, but I can understand that you have enough to do without extra trouble and expense. Anyway, should any kind friends wish to send, please let them do so.

We are two miles from trenches, and shall be going in on Sunday. A few shells are knocking round, but we take no notice and sleep well. Well, don't worry. We are in comfortable billets and with very decent fellows, and they have shared their bread, etc., with us.

I shall not attempt to picture Sydney Baxter's daily life in the terrible salient of Ypres in any detail, but that I may prove my words that he was a typical soldier let me quote just one letter received at this time.

My own Dear Mother,

I have not been able to write before as we have just come out of the trenches after being there since Monday. Thanks very much for sweets and letters. They are very acceptable indeed. Thanks for P.O. We have now been paid, and so shall be all right. Chocolates, handkerchiefs, etc., are fine. Neither George nor I felt anything peculiar when coming under fire as I expected we should. We were all right in the trenches, which are very good indeed. They are a bit different to what I expected, but of course they vary. It seems to me safer to be in the trenches than out; however, it is bad luck if you are hit. No one was killed in our company all the time we were in, and only three wounded, so you will see there is not much to worry about; and with some pay and parcels which I have received, and about twelve letters, I feel much better.

Sydney Baxter often mentions his chum in this record and I think the following extract from George's letter about this time may well be inserted here. The two boys were inseparable until the last and absolute bodily separation between the living and the dead.

Everything is going on all right with us. We have finished our first taste of trench life, and on the whole it was rather enjoyable. We went in last Monday and came out late on Saturday. The first two or three days were wet, so our opportunities for sleep were few, especially as at our part of the trench there were no dug-outs and our sleep had to be obtained in the open air. In fact, until the fourth day I only had one hour's sleep, and on the last day I managed about five hours. The chief trouble was trying to boil water, but we managed by cutting a candle into small pieces and putting this, with a piece of rag, into a tin, using the rag as a wick.

Our five days and nights were on the whole fairly quiet; in fact, during the day hardly any shots were exchanged, most of the firing being done at night. During the day it was impossible to look over the trench, as we were only fifty yards from the Germans, so we considered it advisable not to exhibit too much curiosity in case our health suffered thereby. At night time the Germans use star-shells to illuminate the proceedings, and they always seem nervy and think we are going to attack their trench. If we start firing a little more than usual they think it is the signal for an attack, and they blaze away like fury. We had a good example of this on our last night in the trenches.

Someone started firing, someone else took it up and in no time the noise was like the final end-up of fireworks at the White City. From that it got much worse, and I suppose they really thought we were going for them, so their artillery sent us a few shells; but they did no damage. Eventually they seemed satisfied that we were quite safe, so they wound up the proceedings.

There is one lot here who, whenever they go into the trenches, shove their hats on their rifles, wave them about, and then shout across to the Germans to come out in the open and have a proper fight. Whenever this happens the Germans lie low and hardly fire a shot.

"One advantage of being so close to the Germans is that they cannot shell us without damaging their own trench as much as ours, so that, although we heard plenty going along overhead, we had none very near us.

CHAPTER 5

One Young Man at Hill 60

Many have described in vivid, and none in too vivid, language the fighting in the spring of 1915. This one young man went through it all, through the thickest of it all. He can tell a tale which, if written up and around, would be as thrilling as any yet recorded of those heroic days. But I prefer, and I know he, a soldier, would prefer, to chronicle the events of his day after day just as they occurred, without colour, and without comment.

I print, then, Sydney Baxter's account of the fighting as he wrote it. I promised that this should be an altogether true chronicle, and it is well that some who live in the shelter of other men's heroism should know of the sacrifices by which they are saved. And then, too, as I read his pages, I heard a suggestion that we were all in danger of "spoiling" the wounded who come back to us after enduring, for our sakes, the pains he here describes.

For three nights the bombardment had been tremendous.

It was 7 o'clock on the Sunday morning when we first got the alarm—'turn out and be ready to march off at once.' We heard that the Hill—the famous Hill 60—had gone up and that we had been successful in holding it, but the rumours were that the fighting was terrific. We were soon marching on the road past battered Vlamertinghe. Shells of heavy calibre were falling on all sides, and we made for the Convent by the Lille gate, by a circuitous route—round by the Infantry Barracks. We dumped our packs in this Convent, where there were still one or two of the nuns who had decided to face the shelling rather than leave their old home.

We were sorted up into parties. Our job was to carry barbed

wire and ammunition up to the Hill. I was first on the barbed-wire party; there were about fifty of us and we collected the 'knife-rests' just outside the Lille gate, and proceeded up the railway cutting. Shells were falling fairly fast, as indeed they always seemed to along this cut. At last we got our knife-rests up by the Hill and dumped them there. Fortunately we had very few casualties. We started to go back, but, half-way, we were stopped at the Brigade Headquarters, a badly damaged barn, and were told that we had to make another journey with bombs. We were just getting a few of these bombs out of the barn when the Boches landed three shells right on top of it. Many of our men were laid out, but we had to leave them and try to get as much ammunition out as possible. The barn soon caught fire, and this made the task a very dangerous one indeed. Every minute we were expecting the whole lot of ammunition to go up, but our officer had already taken a watch on it and gave the alarm just a few seconds before the whole building went clean up into the air.

We then began to retrace our steps along the railway out to the Hill. Each man carried two boxes of bombs. Just as we reached the communication trench, leading on to the Hill itself, the Boches sent over several of the tear-gas shells. We stumbled about half-blind, rubbing our eyes. The whole party realised that the boys holding the Hill needed the bombs, so we groped our way along as best we could, snuffling and coughing, our eyes blinking and streaming. We stood at intervals and passed the bombs from one to the other, and had nearly completed our job when the word came down that no one was to leave the Hill, as a counter-attack was taking place a few minutes before 6 o'clock. We had then been at it for nearly ten hours. By this time the bombardment from both sides was stupendous; every gun on each side seemed concentrated on this one little stretch, on this small mound.

Six o'clock came and I heard a shrill whistle and knew that our boys were just going over the top. Immediately there was a deafening rattle of machine guns and rifle fire. And then a stream of wounded poured down this communication trench. The wounds were terrible, mostly bayonet. None were dressed; there had been no time, they were just as they had been received. Many a poor chap succumbed to his injuries as he staggered along our trench. To keep the gangway clear we had to lift these dead bodies out and put them on the top of the parapets. It was ghastly, but you get accustomed to ghastly things out here. You realise that fifty dead bodies are not equal to one living. And these poor fellows, who only a few minutes before had been alive and full of vigour, were now just blocking the trench. And so we simply lifted the bodies out and cast them over the top.

By this time the trench was absolutely full of wounded, and our little party was told to act as stretcher-bearers, and to get the stretcher cases down. We were only too glad to do something to help. The first man that my chum and I carried died half-way down the cutting. We felt sorry for him, but could do nothing. He was dead. So we lifted his body on to the side of the track and returned for the living. This work lasted some considerable time, and when more stretcher-bearers came up, most of the cases had been carried down, so we returned to the Convent exhausted, nerve-shaken, and very glad of the opportunity of a few hours' sleep.

The sights we had seen, the nerve-racking heavy shelling had upset our chaps pretty badly. Many of them sobbed. To see and hear a man sob is terrible, almost as terrible as some of the wounds I have seen—and they have been very awful. However, as quite a number of the men had only recently come out, it was natural enough that we should be upset by this ordeal. Time and repeated experiences of this kind toughen if they do not harden a man—but for many this was the first experience.

Early the next morning the whole battalion made a move nearer to the Hill. For the greater part of the day we stood to in dugouts on the side of the railway embankment, but at dusk we lined up and received instructions as to the work we had to do that night and the following day. Our officers told us that we were going to the Hill to hold off all counter-attacks, and that if any man on the way up was wounded no one was to stay with him. He must be left to wait for the stretcher-bearers. Every man would be needed for the coming struggle, and although it seemed almost *too* hard that one must see his chum struck down and be unable to stop and bind up his wounds, there was no doubt that the order was very necessary.

We started off in single file by platoons. This time we did not go up the cutting, but made our way round by the reservoir and the dilapidated village of Zillebeke. The first man to go down was one of my own section. We remembered the order not to stop, although the temptation was very strong. So we left him, wishing him the best of luck and hoping that he would soon be in Blighty.

After this the casualties came faster and faster as we entered into the shell-swept area. The machine guns were sweeping round and were making havoc in our ranks. Gradually we drew near to the little wood just beside Hill 60, and were told to occupy any dug-outs there until further orders. It was at this time that the whizz-bang shell made its debut. We had not encountered this kind of shell before; it was one that gave absolutely no warning and was used for quite small ranges.

We had been in these dugouts for about half an hour when we were told to fall in and each man to carry two boxes of bombs. We then went into the communication trench of the old front line. At this stage our company commander was wounded.

However, we got on to the Hill, and each man was detailed— some for firing, some for bombing, and some for construction. All the trenches were blown in entirely, and a large number of us, including my chum and myself, were detailed for this construction work. Under heavy shelling we tried to build up the blown-in portions of the trenches. This was just at a corner leading right on to the Hill and part of our old front line. We laboured here all night through. Just before dawn the shelling increased, and the bombardment grew very terrific.

All possible were rushed up into the crater to take the places of the fallen. Casualties were terrible, and the wounded came past our corner in one stream; several of my own friends were amongst them, and two of them, who had come out with me, were killed just a few yards away. This terrific cannonade continued until dawn, when things quietened down a little. Every one's nerves were on edge, and all of us were thoroughly tired out. In every part of the trench lay numbers of dead bodies; in fact, to move about, one had to climb over them. I sat down, dead beat, for some time on what I thought was a sandbag. I discovered afterwards it was a dead body.

Shortly afterwards we were relieved by another regiment, and in small parties of tens made our way back into Ypres. This was done in daylight, and we were spotted and shelled by the Boches. However, we were only too glad to get away from that ghastly hell, and literally tore along the hedges down past the reservoir into Ypres. At the hospital, at the other end of the town, the remnants of the battalion were collected, and it was there that Sir Horace Smith-Dorrien spoke to us, congratulating our battalion on its stand the night before. Worn out, we lined up and marched back along the road to Vlamertinghe, fondly imagining we were going back to our well-earned rest (as a matter of fact that was the programme), but we had not been in these huts more than half an hour when down the road from St. Julien there rushed one long column of transports, riderless horses, and wounded (mostly of the French Algerian regiments). And everywhere was the cry, 'The Boches have broken through!'

Orders were soon forthcoming, and we turned out, loaded magazines, and marched off in the direction from which the Boches were supposed to be coming. On our way up many dispatch riders passed, and each one had the same comforting message—'The Canadians are holding them.' We went no further, but received orders to dig ourselves in across the road, and that in the event of the Boches getting as far as this we were to hold them until the last man. Fortunately the splendid Canadians had not only held their ground, but with terrible losses had pushed the enemy two or three miles back; had, in fact, practically regained all the ground lost.

At nightfall we drew picks and shovels and made our way in the direction of St. Julien. We got to the Yser Canal, and in crossing the bridge met the batch of wounded coming back. This was not heartening, but certainly gave all of us a keener desire to get to grips. On the side of the banks of the Yser we were formed into three waves and received instructions that we were going over in extended order to drive the Huns from the position. But the Canadians had done so grandly that we were not needed until the following morning, when, in broad daylight, the remnants of the once whole battalion, in single file, made their way along the hedges, taking advantage of every possible cover, up to the village of St. Jean.

Much to our surprise we did not stop there, but went right through and came within view of the Boches. Immediately we were under the special care of their artillery, and within a short space of time lost half of our numbers. We had to dig ourselves in with entrenching tools, but after having got fairly decent cover, had to move on again over to the left. We got right forward into the front line, and found it held by a mere handful of the Canadians, who received us with enthusiasm and were so heartened by our reinforcements that they were more determined than ever to hang on to the last.

Meanwhile between the two lines our wounded lay unattended, those who were able made their way, crawling and rolling through the barbed wire, into our lines. At dusk half of the Canadians occupying the trench made one rush after another to bring in their wounded and helpless comrades. It was a wonderful sight. Again and again these fellows went out, each time carrying back a wounded man. I was the extreme end man of our regiment, and so was right next to the Canadians themselves. Their officer, who was hit some time during the evening, came back with his arm in a sling, refusing to go down the line to the dressing station, as he preferred to stay with the remnants of his company. He was a most encouraging chap, and it was here that I noticed the difference between the companionship of these officers and men and those of our own army. The ordinary private would pull out his small packet of Woodbines and offer one to his officer, who would accept it with the same feeling of gratefulness as he would a cigar from a brother officer.

We stayed with these Canadians for two days. For some reason or other the transport had failed to bring up our rations, but we did not suffer for lack of food, for whatever the Canadians had, we had too. They shared with us all their rations and kept us for those two days.

At the end of that time, during which we had witnessed several attacks on the right, we were relieved from those trenches and marched back to the farm on the other side of the Canal. But it was not for a rest; for every night we had to go up digging and consolidating the trenches regained and digging communication trenches.

It was on one of these digging fatigues that my chum was killed. He and I had been given a small sector to dig, and it was really a fairly quiet night, as far as firing was concerned. We had dug down a depth of about three feet and had secured ourselves against rifle fire and were putting the final touches to our work, which we had rightly viewed with pride and satisfaction, when the order came—'D Company file out towards the left.' We were terribly disappointed for we had worked all that evening on digging ourselves in here and we knew that it meant a fresh start elsewhere. We were just clambering out when there rang out one single shot from a sniper, apparently lying in front of the German lines.

We all got up with the exception of my chum. I did not for a minute imagine he had been hit, but merely thought he was making sure that the sniper had finished, so I touched him—and he half rolled towards me. I lifted him up and said, 'Did you catch it?' All he could do was to point to his chin. He was an awful sight. A dum-dum or explosive bullet had caught his jawbone and had blown the left lower jaw and part of the neck away. I realised at once that it was hopeless, for it took four bandages to stop the spurting. One of our fellows ran off for the stretcher-bearers. One of these came back, but he could not stop the flow of blood at all, and the corporal said, 'No good: it will all be over in a minute.' I could not believe it at all—it did not seem possible to me that George with whom I had spent every hour, every day in close companionship for so many months past, was dying.

The party went on and I was left alone, but I risked all chances of court martial and stayed with my wounded friend. I couldn't leave him until I was absolutely certain that he was past all aid. He did not last very many minutes, and I knelt there with my arm round his shoulders, hoping against hope that something could be done. He was called to pay the supreme sacrifice of all. And with just one gasp he died.

I was in a terrible condition. My clothes were soaked in blood, my hands all red, my mind numbed. Nothing could be done, so I went and joined my company, but first made application to the sergeant-major that I might help to bury my chum. This was granted, and as three other men were killed that evening, a party of us were detailed to make graves for them. I can see now those four graves in a square, railed off by barbed wire, on the cross-roads between St. Jean and St. Julien. On one corner stood an estaminet and trenches ran all round. A chaplain was passing, and we had a service of a minute or two. The time was about 2 o'clock on Saturday morning. We were only able to dig down a couple of feet, and these graves must, I fear, have suffered from the heavy shelling which followed, but I like to think that my chum still rests there undisturbed.

How I got back to the barn that night I do not know. I certainly was not my natural self, and it was more a stagger than a march. It was impossible to realise that I should see George no more. And on the following day I had to face the still harder task of writing to his parents and to the girl he had left behind.

To this, written by Sydney Baxter, I add nothing. Not to me has it come to dig a shallow, shell-swept grave for my chum. What words, then, have I?

CHAPTER 6

One Young Man Receives a Letter

George's stepfather wrote to Sydney Baxter as soon as he received the heartbroken letter telling of his chum's death. To this letter from the father I devote a chapter. It must stand alone. In all the glorious annals of the war it is, to me at least, unique. Nothing that I can write can add to its pathos or increase its heroism or enhance its beauty. I leave it to speak for itself—this letter which will live, I believe, as the most beautiful expression of a stepfather's love and devotion in our language.

My dear Laddie,

Our hearts are breaking for you, and our thoughts and prayers are much taken up on your behalf. All along we have united you and George in our petitions, and all that was sent addressed to George was meant for Syd and George. We never thought of you separately at all, but just as sure as you shared all in common, so our thoughts were for you both.

George's call home was undreamt of by me. It was dreaded by his mother, but I hardly think the possibility of such a thing had entered into the minds of his sisters or brothers. I cannot explain it, but I never expected him to give his life out there. I knew many were praying for you both, and must have rested my mind completely on the expectation of our prayers being answered in the way we wanted. It was not to be. And at the first look one feels rebellious in that God permitted his death to take place. But who am I, and of what account am I, in the scheme of things? Can I understand the infinite thought of God? Can I see the end, as He can? I can only bow my head, with a heart full of sadness, and accept the ruling of my God;

and hope for a reunion with our dear lad when my call shall come.

It was something for me, a stepfather, to have had the fathering of such a dear lad. It is a heart-break to me that that is ended, and never more in reality (though I expect often in mind) shall I hear his voice or feel his kiss, or see the dear lad, as he used in these later years to do, standing in front of the fireplace talking down at me on the chair or listening to me talking up at him on Saturday nights. You can picture him, I have no doubt. Now all is over, his place in the home is empty—but in the heart that can never be. His Mum (as he always called his mother) is heart-broken, but very brave. The dear woman is worthy to have had such a son, and that is praise indeed. If she was prouder of one of the children or made any distinction between them, George held that place, and though I think we were all con-scious of it, none of us grudged it him. And that is the greatest tribute that could be paid to him—when you think it out. We are all jealous of Mother's love. We all want it, and if one is first he must be good indeed if it is not a cause of trouble. And that it never was in his case.

Now, my dear lad, I have a proposal to make to you. We re-ceived some money to send things out to the lads at the front, and there is some left. Besides, George sent some home, so that he might get what he wanted sent him without asking if I could afford it, I suppose. Well, I am to send you some little thing every now and then; you are to get another friend and share with him, and you are to make every endeavour short of cowardice (of which you are not capable) to save your life, valuable to all who have the privilege of knowing you, doubly valuable to your mother, and precious to your many friends. We feel we have a personal claim on you, and I am writing you just as I would were you indeed my boy, and we entreat you to bear up, to do your duty, to be a brave and true and Christian lad, and to come back safe to us all. Oh, what a happy day it will be when we welcome you back home!

We shall always think of you as partly ours; and for what you were to and did for George we will ever bless you. Dear lad, get another friend to lean upon and be leant upon. It is a glorious thing—friendship. You risked your life to try and save George's. God bless you for it. I think He will. If you could read our hearts, you would feel afraid. I cannot write as I would like. It is in my heart, in my brain, but the pen won't put in on the paper. It couldn't. But it is there, a deep love for you, a great admiration for your bravery, and an earnest prayer that you may be preserved to live a happy and useful life for many years to come.

Mummie wishes me to say how her heart goes out to you, and how she feels for you in your loneliness. Be assured of a place in a good woman's prayers, and be assured also that all of us continue constantly in prayer for you. We did not know how constantly and continually we could petition the Great Father till you lads went away. We will not cease because one needs them no more. Rather we will be more constant, and perhaps that may be one of the results of this war. Think what a power the prayers of a whole world would have with God! If only they were for the one thing—that His Kingdom would come, it would be accomplished at once! May the knowledge of His all-pervading love dwell more and more in the hearts of the people of the world, so that wars and all kindred evils may cease and the hearts of the people be taken up with the one task of living for God and His Kingdom.

May God be ever present with you, watching over and blessing you, and may He come into your heart more and more, helping and sustaining you in your hard task, and blessing you in all your endeavours to be His true son and servant.

    Your loving friend,

G—— B——.

P.S.—We have not, up to the time of writing this, received an official notification of our poor laddie's death. I felt I must write you, however. You will perhaps be able to read into my letter what I have been unable to say, but all my thoughts for you are summed up in 'God bless you.' Thank all the dear lads for their kind sympathy with us.

CHAPTER 7

One Young Man in the Salient

The city of Ypres, which Sydney Baxter had entered some few months previously, was now a heap of ruins. The whole country was desolate: the once picturesque roads lined by trees were now but a line of shell holes, with here and there leafless, branchless stumps, seared guardians of the thousand graves. On June 7th, 1915, Sydney Baxter writes:

> We have been having a very lively time, a second touch of real life-destroying warfare. Many of the boys have been bowled over. We have had a series of heavy bombardments—shells everywhere, so that it was a matter of holding tight where we were. However, I was again fortunate, and have proved to myself and to the Captain that I can hold my head whilst under heavy shell and rifle fire, although it's impossible to keep one's heart beating normal under such conditions.
>
> We are now entrenched for a day or two, but it is not overlively. A corporal who was a fellow bedman of George's and mine at Crowborough has just been killed. The poor chap died in agony.
>
> It is indeed comforting to know that so many are petitioning 'Our Father' to spare me, if it be His will, through all the dangers and hardships of this uproar, and the confidence that the friends have in my return is very helpful. I have had the feeling that God will give me another chance of doing more work, but the thought of being killed has not the terror it had. The idea of joining George perhaps gives this comfort, but of course I know that it does not rest with me—unless of course by negligence.

Will you include, please, two fat candles as you sent before.

June 16th, 1915.

My Dearest Mother,

Just a short note in reply to yours received this morning. I am still as per usual. Depends on how much sleep I get as to how I feel. As I was able last night to get to bed before 3 o'clock, and slept on to 10 o'clock this morning, I am A1.

We got drenched the night before last—everyone soaked to the skin. We came out of the trench, and as there were no huts or dugouts ready for us, we had to stand out in the rain for over an hour when we arrived at our destination. As the weather changed next day we managed to dry our things. It was a funny sight to see chaps walking about in pants, and some with sandbags for trousers.

It is rumoured we are leaving here to go ——, but being a rumour it won't come true. However, I shouldn't mind a change. We are all fed up with this spot.

The Alcove Dugout,
July 8th, 1915.

. . . How I long to be within the walls of our dear old church! Some of the fellows can't realise or understand when I tell them my church life and work are so much to me. I owe all my happiness to God through my home and to the associations and work at the church. I hope it will be His Divine Will to spare me for fuller activities and to make up for the sins of omission.
" ... Don't imagine for a minute we learn French out here. We rarely see a civilian, and when we do we say, '*Avez vous du pain?*' and the reply is generally 'How many do you want?' They know more English than we do French.

Later.

The fight for Hill 60 and the struggle with the Canadians against the Hun at St. Julien has weakened our division, and we are to be transferred further south to a quieter part of the line.
"We are not sorry, for we feel sadly in need of a rest, and Ypres and its environments are *literally* a shell-swept area of countless graves. The H.A.C. has relieved us, and we marched back the other night to huts a few miles behind the line. The following evening we marched still farther back, crossing the Franco-Belgian border to the rail-head. We are having a few days' rest,

spending many hours cleaning up, not only our clothes and equipment, but our ceremonial drill and exercises.

CHAPTER 8

One Young Man's Sunday

July 25th, 1915.

To tell you that I am at present on this Sunday afternoon lying on the grass watching a cricket match no doubt seems strange. But that is what I am doing—and with quite an easy conscience.

We are some miles from the firing line in a fair-sized French town. It's a treat to be away from the noise of battle, and from sleepless nights, and in a civilised place again. We are only here for a day or two, however, and then on we go—or at least that is the rumour.

We had Church Parade at 10 o'clock this morning, followed by a route march, and so we are free this afternoon.

Two matches are now in full swing, 13 and 15 *v.* the transport, and 14 and 16 *v.* the new platoons. The platoons have licked them by 30 runs, 61 to 31 runs. I may say my interest keeps wandering from the letter, although no slight to you is meant.

"Now please don't think that Sunday is taken up entirely with cricket matches and things of that sort. When the *Padre* can get round to our battalion there is always a service on the Sunday. Sometimes a full-blown Church Parade, like this morning, but these are not what we call Sunday services. The real Sunday services are voluntary ones, either in the open or in a Y.M.C.A. hut. The fellows that go—and there are quite a large number—really go because they feel the need of such a service—not because it is a parade and they *must* turn out.

Our *Padre* has been able to get round to us about every Sunday, when we have been out of the trenches. He is a very broad-minded chap—is not shocked to see us playing cricket on Sundays, for he realises that whilst on rest men *must* have exercise and enjoyment, whatever the day may be. I asked him once whether he would feel justified in playing a footer or cricket match on a Sunday, and he said that if he had been in the trenches for several days, and the day that he came out happened to be a Sunday, he would certainly play.

The services are generally held about 10 o'clock in the morning. We simply go down and enter the hut or tent and take our seats. There is nothing formal; the *Padre* is sure to be there first, and he sits about and has a chat with each man before the service begins. The hut is more or less divided by a curtain or something like that, which separates the service from the part given up to refreshments, and we generally sit round in a circle. There is no set form of worship, and even the hymns are not settled beforehand. The *Padre* just says, 'Well, boys what shall we have?' and the men ask for their favourites, mostly the old-fashioned hymns, such as 'Abide with Me' or 'Rock of Ages.' Then follows a Bible reading and then more singing of hymns. The sermon is generally more of a chat than anything else. The *Padre* does not take a text, but talks of the troubles and difficulties of the day in the most practical manner. I remember one talk I heard on swearing, and another on drinking. The *Padre* didn't preach at us, he did not condemn us at all. He just gave good, sound, hard reasons as to why we should not do these things. These friendly chats with their sound common sense do us far more good than hundreds of stereotyped sermons.

The service finishes up with many more hymns and the Benediction. But even then we do not leave. This particular *Padre* of ours has introduced what he calls 'get-away-from-the-war chats.' We sit round and talk about everything in general—of home, of books, and all general topics. His idea is that we should try to forget about the war for that brief half-hour or so. These talks are very popular; we get large 'congregations,' and these services really do much more good than the official Church Parade, when the battalion often has to stand in the cold for about an hour on end before the service commences.

To this description of religious services at the front Sydney Baxter adds the following note. You will remember that he writes of what he himself has seen and felt. He has fought in the trenches, and we who have not, have got to face life from his point of view if we are to understand and help him in the days to come.

The majority of the men who used to attend these services would probably shock the ordinary church-goer. These chaps would occasionally swear, at times they certainly got too 'merry.' But this did not make them any the less good fellows. Unless one has actually been at the front, it's no good arguing with him or trying to make him understand the front's point of view. What man who has not been through it can even dimly imagine the after-effect of continuous bombardment and heavy shelling? This I do want to say: the whole time these men were at the services they were far more reverent than many I have seen in churches in England. On leaving they would probably speak of the Chaplain as a *damn*, or even more expressive, fine chap; half an hour after the service one might find them playing cards, later on taking rather more than was good for them at the café, and yet there was absolutely no doubt as to their earnestness and sincerity or their attitude towards religion. On the whole they were a far cleaner-living lot of men than those one unfortunately sometimes finds in a place of worship in England.

They were real good sorts. They would never go back on a pal.

CHAPTER 9

One Young Man on Trek

It was on August Bank Holiday Monday that Sydney Baxter's battalion made its long journey south. He writes:

We were up at 2 o'clock that morning, and for two solid hours were loading up the trucks with our transport, G.S. wagons and limbers. It was real sport and we thoroughly enjoyed it. A long row of flat trucks was lined up, and as each limber drew up the horses were unharnessed and we ran the limber right along the whole line of trucks until all were filled. The work completed, we detailed for our trucks. Every trenchman knows those trucks neatly ticketed:

40 *Hommes.*

8 *Chevaux.*

Forty of us packed into a van did not permit even sitting down, and we were very tired after our exertions, but the change of surroundings and the knowledge that we were for a time far away from the reach and sound of shells was sufficient to keep us merry and bright. The journey was very slow, and when we reached Calais it was just twelve hours since we had had a breakfast cup of tea. A few of us decided to run up to the engine and get some hot water and make some tea on our own, but the majority hadn't got any tea tablets or cocoa, and we hadn't enough to go round at a sip each. The cookers were tightly packed on a truck at the rear, and there was no hope from that quarter. And then once again, just as on other occasions where a chance of a hot mug of tea seemed hopeless, and where we were apparently doomed to a comfortless time, the Y.M. was at hand.

There, as we glided into Calais station, we espied a long cov-
ered-in counter displaying the familiar sign of the red triangle.
The order quickly came down, and was more quickly put into
execution, that men could get out and go to the canteen. I
have never seen such a rush. We were like a disturbed nest of
ants. I wondered how on earth those ladies would cope with
us, but I under-estimated their resources. As we came up we
were formed into a column of four deep, and only a few were
admitted at a time. At the entrance was a pay box. Here we had
our *franc* and 5-*franc* notes turned into pennies, that the exact
money might be given over the counter to save any delay.

When I passed up to the counter in due time, I found that
the first sector was solely occupied in pouring out tea into
our quart mess tins, further along buttered rolls and cakes were
piled high upon large trays, and at the last sector cigarettes of all
varieties, chocolate, and nougat were obtainable. It was a splendid array of good things served by the ladies of our own land.
Though, of course, we needed and enjoyed the hot tea and rolls,
it was as much joy to hear our own tongue so sweetly spoken.
The change from the deep voices of our officers and comrades
thrilled us, reminding us of sisters and sweethearts just a few
miles away, across the Channel, and yet so far off, for there was
little chance of leave for a long time.

What a pretty picture those ladies made in the midst of the
khakied crowd, passing quickly from one to another with a
smile for all! I am sure everyone was over-stocked with chocolates and cigarettes, for we all kept returning to the counter to
buy something just for the sake of a smile or a 'How are you
getting on, Tommy?' from one of our hostesses. The whistle
blew and we all made a rush for our trucks. The ladies stood
in a body at the end of the platform, and as each truck passed
waved and wished us good luck. The noise we made was deafening; we cheered and cheered until the little group of England's unknown heroines on the platform passed from sight.
Our hearts were very full.

And so we passed down into the Somme district, the first English soldiers to hold that part of the line.

Here are a few typical extracts from Sydney Baxter's letters about
this time.

We are at rest after some days of trenches, and of course are not sorry to be able to walk about and get a brush up—apart from the catering side, which you can realise is no small item. The weather has been very good of late; and while we were in the trenches it was fine but cold, which makes life more comfortable. We had a new system of guards and work last time, and it was a treat. *I never enjoyed a spell of trenches as I did that*, although the time spent in work and other duties and guards was nearly twelve hours.

Thanks for chocolate, which found a ready home. Girls are not the only ones who like chocs., judging by the amount that disappears here. Sorry my last letter was censored. I am ignorant of what information I could have given; possibly I had a grumbling mood on and was somewhat sarcastic about the many defects and inconsiderations in army life

Later.

My Dearest Mother,

Just a line to tell you I'm A1. By the time you get this our rest will be over, and we shall be entrenched. Thanks for socks. The stove is going a treat. We finished a fatigue at 4 o'clock this morning and made some porridge. It was great, and of course up in the trench it will be trebly handy. We are taking up two big packets of Quaker Oats, and with the tea, cocoa, coffee, and oxo we ought to do well.

Glad to hear about Herbert's wound. Sounds funny, no doubt, but he's lucky to get back at all, for he was at Ypres and it's hot there.

From a letter to a cousin in the United States.

I have sent you one or two photos which may be of interest, and which may be useful to check the 'strafe Englands' of the German who comes to your office. Ask him, if in these pictures the Huns look as if they believe they're winning, and then compare them with those of our boys and of the Frenchies in the trenches, and with those of our wounded. My! there's just all the difference between them!

I also send a French field service card, so you now have an English and a French one. I'm afraid a Russian card is out of the question, unless I get sent near them in the Balkans; and when I think of that I also think of a ditty that we sing, which runs:

I want to go home, I want to go home,
The Johnsons and shrapnel they whistle and roar;
I don't want to go to the trenches no more.
I want to go home,
Where the Allemands can't get at me,
Oh my! I don't want to die; I want to go home.

You'd better not show this to that German or else he'll believe we *mean* it as well as sing it. We have a rare lot of ditties. We often sing across—'Has anyone seen a German Band,' or 'I want my Fritz to play twiddly bits on his old trombone.' We really have a good bit of fun at times; other days are—crudely, but truthfully putting it—'Hell.' The first month I had out here was such. You heard of Hill 60 back last April, and the second battle of Calais. It was during that time that I lost my friend, with whom I joined. Since we were thirteen years old we've been inseparable. Only 40 per cent. of the draft I was on are left, and in my pocket I have a long list of chums whom I shall never see again in this world. It seems wonderful to me that I should be spared whilst so many better men go. Naturally I am thankful, especially for mother's sake, that I have escaped so far. Only once during the eight months out here have I been more than ten miles from the firing line, and ten miles is nothing to a gun.

Well, now I must knock off for dinner, the variety of which never changes. You've heard of 'Stew, stew, glorious stew'; perhaps, however, beer was the subject then. Well, I'll resume at the first possible moment; for, in the Army, what you don't go and fetch you never see, and then again, first come first served, last man the grouts."

Here we are again; I was last for dinner, but didn't do badly by reason of it. I am writing this at a house which our Chaplain has put at our disposal. It's quite a treat to sit on a chair and write at a table, after sitting on the ground with knees up and a bad light.

The trenches are in a rotten state now owing to the heavy rain and the snow. It's like walking on a sponge about eighteen inches deep. Squelch, squelch you go and not infrequently get stuck; parts are knee deep in water, and icy cold water trickling into your boots is the reverse of pleasant or warm. Then the rain trickles through the dugout roof—that caps it. I really don't think there can be anything more irritating than the drip, drip in the region of the head. Then of course your hands are covered in mud, for as you walk along you need your hands to keep your balance, and the sides are all muddy as well. You come inside then and eat your quarter of a loaf for breakfast and go without for tea—the usual ration is one-third of a loaf, which generally is found sufficient. We get jam, too, and bacon daily, butter three times a week, and stew for dinner every day in trenches or not.

Our sergeant took us to the whizbangs concert party last night. It was A1—one chap makes his fiddle absolutely speak. He played that Volunteer Organist and parts of Henry VIII., the *basso* sang 'Will o' the Wisp,' and most of the other songs were old 'uns. I tell you, you wouldn't believe we had such things a couple of miles behind the line.

On Sunday I went to church. It was the hall that the concert party use. Right glad we were to sing the old hymns again, for we only get one Sunday in two months down here on rest. We had five bandsmen to keep us in tune, and, with a good sermon, the evening was both enjoyable and helpful. Afterwards we came back and I had a discussion with two others on Christianity, the work of the Church, Salvation Army, Y.M.C.A., and other such organisations. It was very interesting, for one of them was an out-and-out atheist who was under the impression that Christians were all hypocrites, cranks, and prigs.

The last extract from a letter to Sydney Baxter's office.

My! I should like to be back working at the business in *any* department. I reckon I shall not be much good the first six months, knowing practically nothing of what has happened since this time last year. However, no doubt, they'll find me a job somewhere. They'll certainly find me very keen. They say this life spoils you for the office, but I shan't be sorry to return to it. Mind you, I feel very much fitter and stronger in eyesight, less neuralgia and headache than before; but I shall go in for more fresh air and bring up the balance that way.

The trenches are in a lively state now, all mud and water; however, now November has come I expect they will generally be in a damper state, and so we shall have to get used to it, as we had to last March.

It has rained every day, and I can tell you we've been very fed up at times. It's hard to see the funny side of things when soaked through, caked in mud, and tired, but we feel different already after a couple of nights in our blankets and a few square meals.

I am keeping very fit, although the last spell knocked me up a bit; but a little rest will do wonders, and I shall be full of fighting strength again and ready for the Hun.

CHAPTER 10

One Young Man Answers Questions

Sydney Baxter's American correspondent has sent me a letter which gives such an admirable picture of the day-to-day life of a Tommy at the front that it merits a separate chapter.

I am glad that you like the idea of Questions and Answers. I should never have thought of explaining some of the things you mention had you not asked. Here goes:

Question No. 1.—How do you find time to write so much? I've often wondered, as I should think you'd want to sleep when out of the trenches.

A.—Well, for one thing, I am very fond of writing letters. To me it's not a bore as it is to some. To me it's a medium by which one can have a nice chat with one's chums (both sexes), and looking at it in that way you can understand. I write to you because I thoroughly enjoy the little talks between us. So much for the inclination, which has much to do with the time, as—where there's a will there's a way. When in the trenches the sentry duty usually runs two hours on, four hours off—all the way through. In addition, we get five hours' work a day. Now the total hours of duty are thirteen out of twenty-four: and as I only need six hours' sleep, that leaves five hours for cooking, eating, reading, or writing. I used to have a programme somewhat like this: rest hours at night—sleep; rest hours before 12 o'clock—sleep; and in the afternoon read or write. Starting from 6 o'clock one evening it works out: 6 to 8 guard, 8 to 10 work, 10 to 12 sleep, 12 to 2 guard, 2 to 6 sleep, 6 to 8 guard, 8 to 10 breakfast and odd jobs, 10 to 2 work, 2 to 6 read and write, and afterwards tea. This will give you a little idea. I have only two meals a day whilst in trenches, and cocoa once in the night.

By the way, when out on 'rest' we sleep up to midday the first day, and as we go to bed at nine o'clock on the following evenings we get plenty of sleep. The chief advantage of 'rest' is the change of food and more exercise, which the officers see we get. Whilst on 'rest,' it's drill, etc., in the morning, sport in the afternoon, letters or reading in the evening.

Q. No. 2.—Is a dugout a hidden structure covered with sandbags where you only sleep, and are there such luxuries as beds? *A.*—I think I could write a small book on dugouts, then leave much unwritten. Let me describe two I have actually been in. My first was on Hill 60. It was a little sand-bag one that stood 3 feet high, 4 feet wide, and 5 feet long. This was shared by eleven of us, who had to take it in turns to sleep. This is the usual type of front-line dug-out. In most cases they are large enough to squeeze all men off duty into them, but of course shells and wet cause them to smash up at times.

Another dugout I have been in was some 20 feet deep with iron bars supporting the roof, and capable of holding one hundred men. This was not in the trenches. It had sticks some 3 feet high, with wire stretched right across, making eight beds. However, I always prefer the ground; the wire beds are narrow and not long enough for me. I'm over 6 feet.

Q. No. 3.—Do you stay in trenches forty-eight hours without ever taking off your boots or resting, and how do you get your food up, etc., if you are on duty all the time? *A.*—When in the firing line a soldier never takes off his boots, clothes, or equipment except for one thing, that is to grease the feet with an anti-frostbite preparation. As for rest, you can see that with one man in three on lookout, you get a little rest, at least six hours, which I found enough. When in a big attack you are of course scrapping all the time.

Rations are carried up by other men who are either on rest or in reserve. As a matter of fact when on rest you are seldom more than three miles away. The rations are carried up in sacks by limbers as far as the transport can take them—it varies according to the level of the ground and activities. These limbers are met by ration parties who carry two sacks each, right up to the trenches. Every sack is marked 'D' for company, '15' for platoon, and so we always get them. We carry an emergency ration of biscuits, bully beef, and tea and sugar in case of accidents. I have only once found it necessary to use mine.

Q. No. 4.—In the battles you have been in, did you come face to face with the Huns, or just shoot at range?

A.—Yes, once when we were driving them back, and once when they were advancing. Apart from that it has been shooting when a head shows. The nearest I've been in a trench to the Hun was 15 yards, but most of them range from 60 to 150 yards. You see we are a rifle regiment and so do not do many charges, but occupy places for sniping, and relieve the line regiment after it has charged, and by the rifle fire keep the Hun from counter-attacking.

Q. No. 5.—How do you get posts—are carriers in danger?

A.—The letters are put in the ration sacks. The party often get some killed or wounded.

Q. No. 6.—Do you get acquainted with French civilians, and have you picked up any of their language?

A.—There are a few civilians in the deserted villages near the firing line, and by dint of repetition and purchase I have picked up a little, but I cannot possibly spell it. You see we do not enter towns.

Q. No. 7.—When one series of trenches is built, how does the enemy get a chance to build close to them?

A.—How? Why, under cover of darkness, either by putting a line of men to form a screen and keep up firing with men digging behind, or by digging a trench at right angles, and making a T. The first method is mostly used as it is quicker, but more casualties occur.

Q. No. 8.—Do you have any fear of air raids over the trenches?

A.—No, because a trench is too small an object to be likely to be hit by a bomb dropping from a height. The flying men would very possibly hit their own people instead. However they drop them on our rest billets. We get used to the shells, and this is only another way of presenting them.

Q. No. 9.—What about gas?

A.—They very seldom use it now. Our helmets are so efficient, they cannot do any harm in sending it over. They might catch one or two who were slow in getting their helmets on, but we have gongs to give warning.

CHAPTER 11

One Young Man's Leave

He again writes:

We had done two days out of our six in the trenches a little south of Albert. They were in such a state that it was impossible to walk from one post to another. The mud was over our knees and all communication was cut off by day. At night we fetched our rations, water, and rum by going over the top—a little sought-after job, for Fritz was most active and cover scarce. I had just finished my two hours at the listening-post, and had crawled into my dug-out for a four-hour stretch. It was bitterly cold, and although I had piles of sandbags over me I couldn't get warm, and, like Bairnsfather's 'fed-up one,' had to get out and rest a bit. Two hours of my four had passed when word came down that I was wanted by the sergeant-major. Hallo, thinks I, what am I wanted for? Ah, letters! I was a source of continued annoyance to the captain because of my many letters.

However, he that expecteth nothing shall receive his seven days' leave, for that's what it proved to be. I stood with unbelieving ears whilst the serjeant-major rattled off something to the effect that I was on the next party for leave, and was to go down H.Q. the following night. I crawled back to my dugout, wondering if I was really awake. Eventually reaching our post, I cried, 'John, my boy, this child's on a Blighty trip.' No profuse congratulations emanated from that quarter, but a voice from a dug-out cried, 'Good! you can take that clip of German cartridges home for me.' This was our souvenir hunter; he'd barter his last biscuit for a nose cap of a Hun shell, and was a frequenter of the artillery dugouts. My next two hours' guard was carried out in a

99

very dreamy sort of way. I had already planned what I should do and how I would surprise them all. Next day I was busy scraping off the mud from my tunic and overcoat. I spent hours on the job, but they seemed very little different when I had finished.

That night I covered the three miles of mud and shell-holes to H.Q. in record time. There I met the other lucky ones and received orders to turn in and parade at 9 a.m. for baths and underclothing. There were no trousers, puttees, or overcoats in the stores, and so we had to come over as we were, a picture that had no fitting background other than the trenches. At dusk we boarded the motor-bus which conveyed us to the rail-head. That old bus had never had such a cargo of light hearts when plying between Shepherd's Bush and Liverpool Street. At the rail-head we transferred to the waiting train, and it was not long before we were on our way. Bully beef and biscuits were on the seats, our day's rations. Never mind—we shall soon be having something a good deal more appetising. We did wish we had something warmer than the water in our bottles, and at our next stop we found our old benefactors. This was another platform canteen, and we were able to refresh ourselves for the remainder of the journey, which was all too slow.

Two R.F.A. and one A.S.C. man shared the carriage with me up to London. We did not speak at all, we were far too much occupied with our thoughts and visions of our welcome. It was Sunday, and there were very few people about when we got in. I clambered out of the carriage prepared to rush to the Bakerloo, when a voice at my elbow asked, 'Is there anything I can do for you? Are you a Londoner?' and a host of questions bearing on my future actions. It was a Y.M. official. He took me to the little box where my *francs* were converted into English coin, then to Bakerloo Tube Station, got my ticket, and with a handclasp dashed off to help another. Had I been bound for the North he would have taken me and given me a dinner, and put me into the right train at the right time. I tell you these Y.M. chaps do their job uncommonly well."

CHAPTER 12

One Young Man Again in the Trenches

On his return from leave Sydney Baxter writes:

January 29th, 1916.

I am writing this in a small *estaminet* which is much overcrowded, and in the conversation can only be described as a din. Madame is hurrying round with coffees and fried *pommes de terre*, whilst *monsieur* is anxiously trying to find out if we are moving tomorrow. He is much disturbed, no doubt thinking of the drop in the number of coffees *après demain*.

I am keeping very fit and well, and much to my surprise have not experienced any of the 'fed-up-ness' I anticipated on my return from leave. To my mind, there is only one experience to equal a leave from Active Service—that is the final home-coming. My leave was pure delight from one end to the other."

Sydney Baxter's Division was soon again on trek to a new position. He writes:

We had stayed in, and passed through, many villages, had even had a fire at one, burning down one or two barns, and yet life was uneventful. Marching most days, or, when billeted, doing platoon drill, playing cards, reading or writing in the cafés or our barns. Company concerts were no good. We had heard all of our soloists' *répertoire*, which was *not* very extensive. There came the day when we marched into Doullens. Strange were the sights of large shops and smartly dressed townsfolk—we were more used to the occupants of obscure villages. The sergeant-major came along with the message, 'Smarten up and keep step through the town.' We needed no bidding.

A soldier doesn't want it, you know, when he becomes the object of admiration and the recipient of smiles from the brunettes of France. On past the Hôtel de Ville we swung—this was a G.H.Q., and 'Eyes left!' was given as platoons passed the guard. Staff officers, resplendent in red-tabbed coats and well-creased slacks, seemed to be showing the populace what fine soldiers they were, while the M.M. Police stood at the corners directing traffic as only the members of that unit can. Into the Rue d'Arras we turned, and outside an *Ecole de Filles* we halted. There was our billet, the best we ever had. In the playground stood our cooker.

Upstairs we were packed into the classrooms, with just enough room allowed to stretch one's legs and to turn over should one wish. We had our stew, and quickly rushed off to see all the town. In the square a military band was playing 'Nights of Gladness,' and we found a crowd gathered round the bandstand, many of them civilians. We stayed and enjoyed the performance, and at the Marseillaise and our own National Anthem every khaki-clad man from private to general stood at attention, and the latter at the salute. It was a grand spectacle, and one felt proud to be a soldier. We went and had a look at the shops and into the church, until nearly 5 o'clock, when we debated amongst ourselves as to whether we should go back for tea or wait till 6 o'clock when the cafés open.

Running into a group who had been endeavouring to break the camera, we asked them what they were going to do. 'Why, go to the Y.M.C.A., of course,' they replied. 'Is there really one here? What luck!' We all followed the guide. It was in a market hall, but liberally placarded with the familiar Red Triangle, and so there was no mistaking it. Like most other canteens of the Y.M. it had a long counter and about twelve small tables. The ever-refreshing cup of tea and the good old English slab cake were in plenty, and we asked for nothing better....

It was quite exciting to sit and have tea at a table. Afterwards there was a concert. The artists were A.S.C. men, and, although very markedly amateur, we enjoyed the evening,[Pg 108] which was decidedly a change from our usual evening of cards. Unfortunately we marched away next day and so were unable to get full advantage from that *depôt*. It was one of the Y.M.'s smaller ventures and lacked many of the usual articles of comfort that their huts are renowned for. However, it served its purpose. Troops were able to procure English cigarettes and chocolates, and at the same time have a good tea and a jolly evening. A toast to the Y.M. should always be drunk in hot tea, for supplying it to us in France. It's one of the chief blessings the Association confers on the army.

The battalion was soon in huts some way behind the firing line. Sydney Baxter writes to one of his friends in the office:

Glad to hear everything is O.K., and that you are still smiling. Thank God for that. Whatever happens, still keep smiling. The greatest tonic out here is to know the girls are working so hard, and all the time willingly and smilingly. We know you all miss the boys as they do you, and to read that our friends at home are enjoying themselves is enjoyment to us. We are out to have the harder tasks, and we want you all at home to have the benefits. That's why we feel so bitter against the Air Raids.

Well now, I am glad to write the usual formula. I am very fit and well, and not having such a bad time; things are fairly quiet this side, but not for long, I hope. Everyone is expecting a move and looking forward to it in the sense that it will help to finish the war.

We have had much rain the last few days, and, as these tiny huts we're in are not waterproof, we wake up in the morning soaked and lying in puddles. It's the limit, I can tell you. However, we are on active service and so are not afraid of H_2O. Now, as to my Eastertide. My Good Friday brought with it duty. I was on Police Picket, much the same as a village policeman. Our duties are to see every soldier is properly dressed with belt and puttees before going out, and that there are no suspicious persons around, that all lights are extinguished by 9.30, etc. It's not a bad job, but on a Good Friday it's tough.

Sunday was as usual,—Church Parade in the morning, and free in the afternoon, when we had a cricket match. Monday was the worst day of all. We were called out at 8.30, and from then to 12.30 had to clean up the roads, scrape mud out of ditches, and make drains in our village streets. Nice occupation, wasn't it? The afternoon was not so bad, but we might have had a holiday. Instead we had to go and throw live bombs for practice purposes. The evening, as usual, was free. That ends my Easter-tide, and in spite of what sounds a far from good one I enjoyed it immensely and count myself lucky to be out of the trenches for it.

I ought to have mentioned earlier that we are in a village behind the firing line, in reserve; we shall be having our turn of trenches in a few days, and so we are making the best of our time out. The weather is glorious, and we are having a good time. I do not doubt that there will be some hard work shortly along the front, but it's difficult to say what will happen. Only the folk in charge know. We only obey, and really it's just as well to be in the dark and so escape the worry beforehand.

The death of his chum George was often in Sydney Baxter's thoughts. He writes:

May 21st, 1916.

I have heard from ——; he also mentions to me the opportunity of revenge. I can quite understand and have felt that a life for a life would wipe out the debt, but when my mind dwells on these things I always try to think what George would have me do, and I know his answer would be: 'Why, the German was only doing his duty. I should have done the same myself.' That is true. We fire, but we little know what suffering we cause. We do our duty and the Germans do theirs. It rests with the Heads as to clean methods or not.

The turn in the trenches soon came, and it was a rough turn too. The following are extracts from letters written to his mother:

June 6th, 1916.

I have been unable to write before, as we have been having an extremely busy and horrible time. From the day we entered the trench till now has been one series of heavy bombardment, an absolute rain of shells everywhere—a whole week of it. How so many managed to come out alive I don't know.

We lost four killed in our platoon, including one of my section, a splendid chap, cool and jolly. Three of us went to see him buried yesterday—we had a short service. His brother is with us, a boy of eighteen, and is naturally very cut up. We have now sixteen graves where there were none a fortnight ago. Ten whom I knew personally are gone—such is war.

All of us have had a shaking up. To many it has been their first dose of real grim warfare, and it has been a sore trial for us to lie out in front with shells bursting all round and no cover. The natural tendency is to run back to the trench and get under cover. However, I managed to pull through, and feel much more confident of myself, and the Captain apparently is pleased, for on the strength of it all I have been made a lance-corporal—only do not yet get paid. That will come later. Of course, this is no big honour, but coming at such a time as this it shows they have some confidence in one's ability.

There are so many senior in front of me that the possibility of further promotion is somewhat remote. One of our majors has got the D.S.O., one of our company lieutenants a Military Cross, and a lance-corporal a D.C.M., and so we have not come out without honour.

I am feeling O.K. myself, and by the time you get this shall be back on a month's rest right away from the line, and until I write again you will know I am out of danger. Your parcel arrived whilst in the trenches, and was very welcome indeed. As far as cash goes, don't worry. Don't send any money, and don't worry; there's no need.

June 8th, 1916.

We are now out on rest right away from our line, in our old village. We are not sorry, as you can imagine, and to sleep in our own little beds once again is lovely. I had a bath this morning, a nice change, and feel quite fit.

Having now my first stripe, I have to go to No. —— Platoon. They are a nice lot of fellows, and I shall be all right there with my old friend, another corporal, while an old section comrade of Crowborough times is platoon sergeant.

As to wants—if you have an old shirt at home I could do with it. But I don't want a new one sent. Also a pair of strong laces, a nail brush (stiff)—that's about all, I think.

June 11th, 1916.

Things are very active along the line, although very little appears in the papers. Our sector has been subject to heavy bombardments, and our first night in the trench saw three separate strafes, and the succeeding days brought a big list of casualties, which by now run well into three figures. The first strafe, which lasted ten minutes according to our artillery observers, brought

1,100 shells of all sizes from the Huns. I was half buried three times, and but for my steel helmet would have had a nasty scalp wound, whereas all that resulted was a dent in the hat and a headache for me.

There follows the last letter Sydney Baxter wrote to his mother before the great Somme offensive. He was facing the possibilities himself and trying to get her to do so too. I have not cared to print this letter in full. Those who have written or received such a letter will understand why.

My Dearest of Mothers,

Owing to increased activity at the front, I hear our letters are to be stopped and only picture, field, and plain postcards can be sent. Therefore you must not worry if you only get such. *If* I can get a letter through *I will*. I do not disguise the fact that things are warmer, for you can read that in the papers, and anything may happen any day.

Thanks for the shirt, laces, brush, cards, and notebook which I received this afternoon; I had just returned after taking a party to another village on fatigue. The P.O.'s have arrived regularly, thanks, dear. I had a good lunch today, steak and chips and fruit after, at a little café where we went this morning. It was O.K.

"As you will have noticed in the papers, our artillery has been very active along the front, and it's when the Hun replies that most of the trouble comes in, for the Huns won't take it quietly for a minute and will send some souvenirs across. It remains to be seen what will happen.

I like my platoon very much, and I have had a very happy time these last few months.

"I often think of the time to come, *après la guerre*, when we shall have the old tea-time chats, a smaller house and less running about for you, of the time when I shall take up my Church secretaryship again and also my work in the City. I wonder what they will put me into?

Well, mother mine, don't worry about me. I'm all right and will be home sooner than you think, even if I last the war through and—I might, you know, unless I get wounded. And if I get that I shall be home sooner, and if I get the only other alternative, well, dear, it's merely a reunion with the others, and a matter of waiting for you. But it remains to be seen.

Well, mother darling, I must now close. I'll drop you both a line every day, so don't worry.

The next line that both received was from a hospital.

CHAPTER 13

One Young Man Gets a "Blighty"

Sydney Baxter's Division was on the left flank of the British attack at Gommecourt, which met with great stubbornness on the part of the enemy, and resulted in heavy losses. He writes:

I was in charge of the 'Battle Police' that day, and we had to accompany the bombers. We started over the top under heavy fire and many were bowled over within a few minutes.

"Lanky of limb, I was soon through the barbed wire and came to the first trench and jumped in. Some seven of us were there, and as senior N.C.O. I led the way along the trench. One Hun came round the corner, and he would have been dead but for his cry '*Kamerad blessé.*' I lowered my rifle, and, making sure he had no weapon, passed him to the rear and led on.

We had just connected up with our party on the left when I felt a pressure of tons upon my head. My right eye was sightless, with the other I saw my hand with one finger severed, covered in blood. A great desire came over me to sink to the ground, into peaceful oblivion, but the peril of such weakness came to my mind, and with an effort I pulled myself together. I tore my helmet from my head, for the concussion had rammed it tight down. The man in front bandaged my head and eye. Blood was pouring into my mouth, down my tunic.

They made way for me, uttering cheery words, 'Stick it, Corporal, you'll soon be in Blighty,' one said. Another, 'Best of luck, old man.' I made my way slowly—not in pain, I was too numbed for that. My officer gave me a pull at his whisky bottle, and further on our stretcher-bearers bandaged my head and wiped as much blood as they could from my face. I felt I could go no further, but a 'runner' who was going to H.Q. led me back. I held on to his equipment, halting for cover when a shell came near, and hurrying when able. I eventually got to our First Aid Post. There I fainted away.

I awoke next day just as I was being lifted on to the operating table, and whilst under an anaesthetic my eye was removed. Although I was not aware of this for some time afterwards I did not properly come to until I was on the hospital train the following day bound for the coast. I opened my eye as much as possible and recognised two of my old chums, but conversation was impossible; I was too weak. The next five days I spent at a hospital near Le Treport. My mother was wired for, and the offending piece of shell was abstracted by a magnet. It couldn't be done by knife, as it was too near the brain.

Thus far Sydney Baxter tells his own story of the great day of his life. I leave it as it stands, though I could add so much to it if I would. Will you picture to yourself this sightless young man, with torn head and shattered hand piteously struggling from those shambles? Will you look at him—afterwards? It's worth while trying to do so. You and I have *got* to see war before we can do justice to the warrior.

The piece of shell which entered his head just above the right eye opened up the frontal sinuses, exposing the brain. "It is wonderful," wrote the doctor who attended him, "how these fellows who have been fighting for us exhibit such a marvellous fortitude." He had lost the end of his fourth finger and another has since been entirely amputated.

To the amazement of all, Sydney Baxter, within a few hours of his operation, asked for postcards. He wrote three—one to his mother, one to someone else's sister, and one to his firm.

This last postcard is a treasured possession of Sydney Baxter's business. It runs as follows:

July 4th, 1916.

Have unfortunately fallen victim to the Hun shell in the last attack. I am not sure to what extent I am damaged. The wounds are the right eye, side of face, and left hand. They hope to save my eye, and I have only lost one finger on hand.

I will write again, sir, when I arrive in England. At present am near Dieppe.

Only lost—that seems to me great.

Above the postcard on the business notice-board the chief wrote:
The pluckiest piece of writing that has ever reached this office.
And by that he stands.

At Treport Sydney Baxter has his last experience of the Y.M.C.A. in France.

One of its members came round the ward, speaking cheery words and offering to write home for us. It sounds a small work, but it was a boon to those of us too weak for even a postcard, or those who had lost or injured their right arms. The nurses are far too busy and cannot do it, and other patients are in a like condition. I always looked out for that gentleman of the Y.M. I was not allowed to read or sit up, and the days dragged horribly. Thursday evening came and many were sent to Blighty. I worried the doctor as to when I should go, and always received the non-committal reply, 'When you are fit to travel.' Saturday, however, found me on board of a hospital ship, and at 9 o'clock that night we arrived at Southampton.

Ant-like, the stretcher-bearers went to and fro, from ship to train. For some reason or other they dumped me in a corner with my head nearest the scene of activities, so that I was unable to interest myself in watching the entraining of others. I feverishly hoped they wouldn't forget me and put me in the wrong train. I was not forgotten by one person, however. He was not an official, not a R.A.M.C. man—no, just a Y.M.C.A. man, ministering to our comfort, lighting cigarettes for the helpless, arranging pillows, handing chocolate to a non-smoker, with a smile and a cheery word for everyone. He asked me where I lived and spoke cheerily to me of soon seeing my mother and friends, and then left on a like errand to another chap. This, as I look back, was typical of all the work of the Y.M.C.A. Its helpers are always at the right place doing the right thing. That is why they have earned Tommy's undying gratitude.

Next day this one young man was being tenderly and graciously cared for in a hospital in Wales. He had finished his bit. To the office he wrote:

July 12th, 1916.
The Hun has put me completely out of action, and I hope within a few months to be amongst you all again—for good, and certainly in time for the autumn session.

The sight of my right eye has completely gone out, but as long as the left one keeps as it is I shall not be seriously handicapped. My glass eye will be an acceptable ornament. The left hand will mend in time; when healed, it will be pushed and squeezed into its original shape. Apart from the wounds I feel very well, and my rapid recovery has surprised all. The first three days in France were critical, and mother was sent for. However, I pulled through and feel as active as ever—at least, I do whilst in bed.

The hole in Sydney Baxter's nut—I use his own phrase—is healing. His hand has been more than once under the surgeon's knife, and he can now wear a glove with cotton-wool stuffed into two of the fingers. He sees fairly well from the unbandaged side of his face.

The chief tells me that Sydney Baxter will have the desire of his heart: he will be "back at business in time for the Christmas rush."

LEONAUR

ALSO FROM LEONAUR
AVAILABLE IN SOFTCOVER OR HARDCOVER WITH DUST JACKET

IRON TIMES WITH THE GUARDS *by An O. E. (G. P. A. Fildes)*—The Experiences of an Officer of the Coldstream Guards on the Western Front During the First World War.

THE GREAT WAR IN THE MIDDLE EAST: 1 *by W. T. Massey*—The Desert Campaigns & How Jerusalem Was Won---two classic accounts in one volume.

THE GREAT WAR IN THE MIDDLE EAST: 2 *by W. T. Massey*—Allenby's Final Triumph.

SMITH-DORRIEN *by Horace Smith-Dorrien*—Isandlwhana to the Great War.

1914 *by Sir John French*—The Early Campaigns of the Great War by the British Commander.

GRENADIER *by E. R. M. Fryer*—The Recollections of an Officer of the Grenadier Guards throughout the Great War on the Western Front.

BATTLE, CAPTURE & ESCAPE *by George Pearson*—The Experiences of a Canadian Light Infantryman During the Great War.

DIGGERS AT WAR *by R. Hugh Knyvett & G. P. Cuttriss*—"Over There" With the Australians by R. Hugh Knyvett and Over the Top With the Third Australian Division by G. P. Cuttriss. Accounts of Australians During the Great War in the Middle East, at Gallipoli and on the Western Front.

HEAVY FIGHTING BEFORE US *by George Brenton Laurie*—The Letters of an Officer of the Royal Irish Rifles on the Western Front During the Great War.

THE CAMELIERS *by Oliver Hogue*—A Classic Account of the Australians of the Imperial Camel Corps During the First World War in the Middle East.

RED DUST *by Donald Black*—A Classic Account of Australian Light Horsemen in Palestine During the First World War.

THE LEAN, BROWN MEN *by Angus Buchanan*—Experiences in East Africa During the Great War with the 25th Royal Fusiliers—the Legion of Frontiersmen.

THE NIGERIAN REGIMENT IN EAST AFRICA *by W. D. Downes*—On Campaign During the Great War 1916-1918.

THE 'DIE-HARDS' IN SIBERIA *by John Ward*—With the Middlesex Regiment Against the Bolsheviks 1918-19.

LEONAUR

ALSO FROM LEONAUR
AVAILABLE IN SOFTCOVER OR HARDCOVER WITH DUST JACKET

FARAWAY CAMPAIGN *by F. James*—Experiences of an Indian Army Cavalry Officer in Persia & Russia During the Great War.

REVOLT IN THE DESERT *by T. E. Lawrence*—An account of the experiences of one remarkable British officer's war from his own perspective.

MACHINE-GUN SQUADRON *by A. M. G.*—The 20th Machine Gunners from British Yeomanry Regiments in the Middle East Campaign of the First World War.

A GUNNER'S CRUSADE *by Antony Bluett*—The Campaign in the Desert, Palestine & Syria as Experienced by the Honourable Artillery Company During the Great War .

DESPATCH RIDER *by W. H. L. Watson*—The Experiences of a British Army Motorcycle Despatch Rider During the Opening Battles of the Great War in Europe.

TIGERS ALONG THE TIGRIS *by E. J. Thompson*—The Leicestershire Regiment in Mesopotamia During the First World War.

HEARTS & DRAGONS *by Charles R. M. F. Crutwell*—The 4th Royal Berkshire Regiment in France and Italy During the Great War, 1914-1918.

INFANTRY BRIGADE: 1914 *by John Ward*—The Diary of a Commander of the 15th Infantry Brigade, 5th Division, British Army, During the Retreat from Mons.

DOING OUR 'BIT' *by Ian Hay*—Two Classic Accounts of the Men of Kitchener's 'New Army' During the Great War including *The First 100,000 & All In It.*

AN EYE IN THE STORM *by Arthur Ruhl*—An American War Correspondent's Experiences of the First World War from the Western Front to Gallipoli-and Beyond.

STAND & FALL *by Joe Cassells*—With the Middlesex Regiment Against the Bolsheviks 1918-19.

RIFLEMAN MACGILL'S WAR *by Patrick MacGill*—A Soldier of the London Irish During the Great War in Europe including *The Amateur Army*, *The Red Horizon* & *The Great Push.*

WITH THE GUNS *by C. A. Rose & Hugh Dalton*—Two First Hand Accounts of British Gunners at War in Europe During World War 1- Three Years in France with the Guns and With the British Guns in Italy.

THE BUSH WAR DOCTOR *by Robert V. Dolbey*—The Experiences of a British Army Doctor During the East African Campaign of the First World War.

CPSIA information can be obtained
at www.ICGtesting.com
Printed in the USA
LVHW042206220423
745096LV00004B/281